AT THE PLACE OF THE LOBSTERS AND CRABS

To Robbie Susan Bulb Coronto
with best wishes

William A Howland

At the Place

of the

Lobsters and Crabs

Indian People and
Deer Isle, Maine, 1605-2005

William A. Haviland

With a Foreword by
James Eric Francis, Sr.

Polar Bear & Company
Solon, Maine
In cooperation with
The Deer Isle-Stonington Historical Society

Polar Bear & Company
P.O. Box 311, Solon, Maine 04979 U.S.A.
207-643-2795 www.polarbearandco.com

First edition 2009
13 12 11 10 09   1 2 3 4 5 6 7
Cover art & design, Emily Cornell du Houx. Frontispiece photo by author.

Library of Congress Cataloging-in-Publication Data
Haviland, William A.
At the place of the lobsters and crabs : Indian people and Deer Isle, Maine,
1605-2005 / William A. Haviland. -- 1st ed.
p. cm.
Includes bibliographical references.
Summary: "An illustrated, anthropological history of the Native American
presence on Deer Isle in Maine, from early seventeenth-century contact
with Europeans to the beginning of the twenty-first century, including the
Etchemins, Mi'kmaqs, Abenakis, Penobscots, the Mawooshen Confederacy,
Passamaquoddies, Maliseets, and other Indian tribes of the Algonquian
language group"--Provided by publisher.
ISBN-13: 978-1-882190-97-3 (pbk. : alk. paper)
ISBN-10: 1-882190-97-1 (pbk. : alk. paper)
1. Indians of North America--Maine--Deer Isle (Town)--History. 2. Indians
of North America--Maine--Deer Isle (Town)--Antiquities. 3. Deer Isle (Me. :
Town)--History. 4. Deer Isle (Me. : Town)--Antiquities. 5. Maine--Antiquities.
I. Title.
E78.M2H38 2009
974.1'45--dc22
2009012761

Manufactured in the U.S.A. by Thomson-Shore, Inc., an employee owned
company—certified by the Forest Stewardship Council and a member of the
Green Press Initiative—using soy ink and acid free, recycled paper of archival
quality, at paper permanence specifications defined by ANSI.NISO standard
Z39.48-992: "The ability of paper to last several hundred years without significant
deterioration under normal use and storage conditions in libraries and archives."

In memory of James B. Petersen:
First student, then colleague, always friend.
It was his paper, *Mawooshen Revisited*, that started the chain
of events that culminated in this book.

Contents

Foreword

In *Space and Place: The Perspective of Experience*, geographer Yi-Fu Tuan puts forth the equation, "space plus culture equals place." Tuan's equation can appropriately be applied to the landscape of the Penobscot Bay region, a space that has little soul or spirit apart from the cultures that have occupied it. No land or region can be fully seen as a place without acknowledging the human element. In *At the Place of the Lobsters and Crabs*, William Haviland weaves a narrative, not just of the space of Deer Isle and adjacent towns, but of a place with heart, soul, and spirit of the cultures that called this place home.

Haviland's training as an anthropologist by itself is not important as a qualification to write a book about a place in Maine. As a scholar Haviland understands history and the people of that place, but more important is the fact that Haviland has deep roots in Deer Isle. The qualification to author a text about a place is a connection to that place. Haviland is unique in that he is a scholar who not only is studying an area and the people there, but his life experience has been shaped by that place and how he perceives it. Haviland's own culture as an American, a Mainer, a scholar with a lifetime connection to Deer Isle all weave together in the tale of a place in Maine and the Native American population that occupied that area over time. Although Haviland is not a Native American, his unique perspective and open-mindedness have crafted a narrative that honors the Maine Native American Wabanaki who have historically occupied this place.

In recent years published stories and histories about the Wabanaki have increased in number. Wabanaki is a term translated as "People of the Dawn," and collectively refers to the Maliseet, Micmac, Passamaquoddy, and Penobscot people who now occupy Maine and the Maritimes and have done so for thousands of years. Although this narrative focuses on Wabanaki people, the geography (place) plays a crucial role in the text.

For thousands of years Wabanaki people adapted their culture to the environments in which they lived. In Maine this environment included coastal lands and islands, as well as inland forests, lakes, and ponds. But the environment is not just limited to the physical space around the culture. The social spaces also have a profound influence on Wabanaki culture. The largest and undoubtedly most difficult adaptation for the Wabanaki was the adaptation to the non-Native American culture that dominates the landscape today. In the face of this foreign culture, Maine Native Americans adapted, survived, and retained a distinct cultural identity in their homeland. This book tells that story in one particular place, Eastern Penobscot Bay.

Today the Maine Native Americans occupy four reservations in Maine. The Maliseet have a community in Houlton, the Micmac in Presque Isle, the Passamaquoddy near Princeton and Perry, and the Penobscot near Old Town. These reservations are only a fraction of a fraction of the ancestral territory of Wabanaki people in Maine.

Areas that are not currently occupied by Wabanaki people still hold stories of Wabanaki occupation. Often these stories are part of the history of colonization and history of Maine. Other times it comes to us in the form of oral traditions handed down from generation to generation. In my study of Wabanaki places in Maine and the Maritimes, I have looked closely at the Wabanaki place names that remain on the landscape. Names such as Passadumkeag, Chesuncook, Penobscot, Kennebec, and Norridgewock, just to name a few, offer us a window into the past of how the ancestors of modern Wabanaki people saw, used, and traveled the land. Place names can be categorized into three groups: First, a geographic or geologic description can be seen in the place name. Secondly, there is land use, or a resource-based description of an area. Lastly, are the legend-based place names. These tend to reinforce the first two categories, but are conveyed through oral story or legend. One such legend is called "Klooscap and the Moose."

"Klooscap and the Moose" is a tale about how the Wabanaki cultural hero, Klooscap, taught Wabanaki people how to hunt for moose. The tale begins in the Moosehead Lake region, where through the slaying of a cow moose and turning her into stone, the story conveys the location and use of Kineo Mountain as a repository for stone to make arrowheads. The story then follows the pursuit of a calf moose to the Penobscot Bay region. It is here that Klooscap slays the calf and the calf's rump, liver, and entrails can be found in that area as distinct landmarks in the bay region. Growing up, I heard this story many times. Not until I visited the landscape in recent years did the true meaning of these areas come into play. Haviland took me on a boat ride in Penobscot Bay to visit the areas called the moose rump, moose liver, and moose entrails, each a distinct Penobscot place name. Visiting that region and understanding the legend highlighted the importance of these places as travel markers. It was clear to me that the legend could be viewed as a navigation map of the Penobscot Bay region. I am thankful to Haviland for this enlightening trip.

Haviland comes to the Penobscot reservation of Indian Island often, a frequent visitor to the Penobscot Nation Cultural and Historic Preservation Department. On one occasion we made arrangements to visit Penobscot Elder Charles Norman Shay at Princess Watahwaso's Teepee Museum. This teepee was formerly a Penobscot gift shop built and operated by Charles' Aunt Lucy Nicolar Poolaw and her husband Bruce. Lucy had a long history in the 1920s as an entertainer and took the stage name Princess Watahwaso. In her honor, and to honor other family members, Charles converted the gift shop into a family museum. Haviland had been conversing with Charles on the phone, but had not been formerly introduced. I had not realized that their paths had crossed years earlier on Deer Isle. Leo Shay and Florence Nicolar Shay, Charles's parents, had visited Deer Isle on occasion when Charles was a child. Charles and his brother had accompanied them. They had visited the island, selling baskets. Haviland had been present as a youth during one of these visits.

Selling baskets to tourists was a way that Penobscots could make a living in the summer months. Like many tribal members, Leo and Florence traveled to many tourist locations, selling baskets and entertaining. Eventually Leo and Florence found a permanent location near the beach on the western shore of Penobscot Bay in the town of Lincolnville. Here they set up a tent to sell brown ash baskets. People traveling US Route 1 through Lincolnville Beach would stop and purchase these items. Bill Haviland had stopped and purchased a pack basket when the shop was in operation.

On the day that Haviland was introduced to Charles Norman Shay at the teepee museum, Haviland presented Charles with that same pack basket purchased decades before. It was one of those moments that make me proud to be a historian. Amidst the beautifully painted murals of Charles' ancestors on the curved interior of the teepee, I witnessed a Penobscot-made pack basket come full circle. This gesture by Haviland speaks volumes of his dedication and sensitivity to Wabanaki people. Charles appreciated Haviland's generosity and displayed the basket prominently in the museum.

When I see that basket today, it reminds that the Wabanaki people, my ancestors, have lived beyond the confines of Indian Island. The Wabanaki culture has shaped the place that we call Maine. Their presence is not just felt in an ancient context, but a historical and contemporary one. Bill Haviland has woven a narrative that brings a contemporary and historical presence of Wabanaki culture to Deer Isle and beyond. This book shows that Wabanaki culture has endured in this place and can be seen as a model for viewing Wabanaki history in other places in Maine and the Maritimes. I am honored to be a part of this important work.

James Eric Francis, Sr.
Tribal Historian
Penobscot Nation

Preface

As one encounters histories of Deer Isle, one gets the impression that, although Indians were here prior to the coming of William Greenlaw around 1760, since then, they have played no part in events unfolding on the island. The fact is, when the first Europeans arrived on the scene, the Indians did not conveniently disappear, but continued to frequent the place right down into the present century. My purpose here is to document their presence and activities over the past 400 years to offset the notion that Deer Isle's history is exclusively that of Europeans and their descendants. The task is not easy, as information is usually fragmentary at best, and often tucked away in odd places. But, scrappy as it is, it affords us glimpses into the lives of Native people. Thus, it serves as a sequel to my booklet, *Deer Isle's Original People*.

Several things came together, quite by chance, that made this project possible. My memories of Deer Isle extend back into the late 1930s, and among them are memories of the Mitchells, the Penobscot family that regularly came to the island to sell baskets and other handcrafted items. Their ancestors are said to have always lived in the region "near the lobsters and crabs," hence the title of this book. I grew up aware as well of the presence of the many shell middens indicative of an ancient Indian presence. Throughout my schooling, Indians always fascinated me, and it was this that led me to anthropology. Ultimately, I spent over 45 years researching, teaching about, and working with various groups of this continent's First Nations. In the course of time, I have learned much, had the privilege of meeting some exceptional people, and formed important friendships.

Among my activities over those years was a good deal of lecturing about the Indians of Vermont, testifying about Native rights in that state before legislative committees and in court, and publication of a major book with a colleague, Marjory Power, called *The Original Vermonters*. Thus, it was natural, upon retirement from teaching, to return to my earliest interests here, and begin pulling together information on Deer Isle's original people. This has led to numerous talks to various local groups, publication of the previously mentioned book on Deer Isle Indians, several guest columns for the local paper, and an exhibit at the Deer Isle-Stonington Historical Society (in collaboration with Marnie Reed Crowell).

As more and more people have become aware of my interests, several have shared anecdotes with me, along with various newspaper clippings, pages from scrapbooks, diary entries, and the like. At the same time, my collaboration with other anthropologists, especially my one-time student and late colleague, Jim Petersen, led me to the discovery of Deer Isle's Indian canoe route, which I had the good fortune to explore from the water with Passamaquoddy historian Donald Soctomah. The final catalyst came when my friends, colleagues and co-authors (of a textbook) Bunny McBride and Harald Prins, in 2003, undertook a project for the National Park Service to produce an historical-ethnographic overview of Native activity in and around Acadia National Park. Over the next couple of years, we shared information back and forth, and at one point I took them, along with Chuck Smythe of the Park Service, around the bay by boat to get a "feel" of the region. Eventually, I was asked to be an outside reviewer of their manuscript. In the course of this the thought dawned on me: "Hey, I can do this for Deer Isle."

The result is this short book. It pulls together a lot of bits and pieces and, for the first 200 years, owes a lot to the work of McBride and Prins, whose explanatory framework I have found essential for making sense of what was going on here. It also owes a lot to all those people who have shared information with me, and who have offered me encouragement along the way. Those who have shared information are acknowledged in the text and/or the section "References Consulted." The encouragement has come especially from Neva Beck, Tinker Crouch, Judy Hill, and Paul Stubing of the historical society, Ann Hooke of Island Heritage Trust, James Eric Francis, Sr. of the Penobscot Nation, Donald Soctomah of the Passamaquoddy Tribe, and my wife, Anita de Laguna Haviland.

I hope that those who read this will consider it a "work in progress" rather than the final word. My gut feeling is that this is the "tip of the iceberg"; my hope is that others will take up the challenge and go on from here.

Deer Isle, Maine   W.A.H.
May, 2009

Acknowledgments

Although I have acknowledged the contributions of numerous individuals in the text, there are others whose assistance needs to be recognized here. To begin, for the sake of completeness, here is the list of all the people with whom I have discussed local Indians.

From the towns of Deer Isle and Stonington: Chandler Barbour, Neva Beck, Carol Billings, Hubert Billings, Lloyd Capen, Tinker Crouch, Althea Eaton, Eugene Eaton, Garfield Eaton, Richard Eaton, John Farrell, Brenda Gilchrist, Alan Gott, Valmore Greenlaw, Carroll M. Haskell, Pamela J. Haskell, Judy Hill, Mayotta Kendrick, Tim Kinchla, Edith Marshall, Veronica Mollek, Callie Parker, Robert Quinn, John Robbins, Paul Stubing, Richard Weed, Connie Wiberg, Elsa Zelley.

From neighboring towns: Genise Chase, Newman Eaton, Ted Hoskins, Julia Lubel, David Webb.

From Indian Island: Carole Binette, James Eric Francis, Sr., Charles N. Shay.

From Pleasant Point: Donald Soctomah.

By correspondence or phone: John Gilchrist (Connecticut), George James (Presque Isle), Bunny McBride (Kansas), Harald Prins (Kansas), Nicholas Smith (Brunswick).

There are at least two others whose names, I regret to say, I did not get: one was the granddaughter of Hilda and Hobart Blake of Harborside, and a woman from Indiana who remembered Gloria Mitchell from summers past in Sunset. I apologize for my oversight, but value their recollections.

My thanks also to the following individuals who read a complete first draft of the manuscript: James Eric Francis, Sr. (Penobscot), Judy Hill (long-time Deer Isle resident), Bunny McBride (anthropologist), Donald Soctomah (Passamaquoddy). I found their comments extremely helpful, and they have made a difference in the final draft. They should not, however, be held responsible for the final product, where any faults are entirely my own.

My thanks also to the Maine Community Foundation for a grant through its Hancock County Fund, Emily and William Muir Fund II, and Ocean Ledges Fund, which made this publication possible.

Finally, thanks to Cindy Longwell of the University of Vermont's Anthropology Department, who did the word processing for me. I am more than grateful for her willingness to take on such a task.

I

The Seventeenth Century

When the first Europeans arrived at Penobscot Bay, they found the region occupied by Etchemins, a people whose homeland stretched along the coast from the Saint John River to the Kennebec. North and east of them lived the Mi'kmaqs, called Souriquois by the French, and (with their eastern Etchemin allies) Tarrantines by the British. South and west of the Kennebec lived the people called Armouchiquois by the French, including the Abenakis and their southern neighbors. Unlike the people who lived north and east of them, who subsisted wholly by hunting, fishing, and gathering a wide variety of wild plant resources, the Abenakis were a people who also grew corn, beans and squash.

Mawooshen and the Mi'kmaq War

By the time the first British sailed into the region, around the start of the 17th century, this distribution of ethnic groups was under stress, triggered by the arrival of Frenchmen in Mi'kmaq country in the 16th century. It did not take long for trade to develop between the two people, with the Natives exchanging furs for European goods including copper kettles (often broken up to fabricate objects of personal adornment or arrow points), cloth, iron axes, as well as guns, powder and ammunition. As this trade intensified, traditional relations with people to the south and west deteriorated; moreover, access to firearms gave the Mi'kmaqs a military advantage over their neighbors. This, and their quick mastery of French shallops*

---

*Open, double-ended vessels, twenty to forty feet long, with a single mast that could not only be sailed but rowed by several men.

Figure 1. Shallops like this one, used by European adventurers in North America, were quickly adopted by Mi'kmaqs, who used them to raid their neighbors along the coast. Drawing by Duane A. Cline, courtesy Harald Prins and Bunny McBride.

(figure 1) allowed them to raid their neighbors along the coast as far afield as Massachusetts Bay. In response, Etchemins east of Schoodic Point, by 1600, had become allies of the Mi'kmaqs. Those west of Schoodic, however, pursued a different strategy; under the leadership of a powerful chief named Bashabas, whose headquarters was at the confluence of the Kenduskeag Stream with the Penobscot River, they created a grand confederacy that included all the local groups of Abenakis as well as Etchemins as far south as Cape Neddick. Called "Mawooshen," the name means "band of people walking or acting together." Reportedly, the confederacy was able to marshal 1500 warriors.

By 1614, the year of John Smith's visit to Penobscot Bay, conflict between the Mi'kmaqs and their allies on the one hand and the Mawooshen Confederacy on the other had become intense, with Isle Au Haut, referred to by Smith as "The Isle of Sorico" (his gloss of Souriquois) perhaps serving as a staging area for the Mi'kmaqs. A year later, Bashabas was killed, and the Mawooshen Confederacy fell apart. No doubt this was abetted by the Great Dying of 1616-18 caused by a disease of European origin that killed off up to 90 percent of local populations. Through all this, Mi'kmaq supremacy continued until the 1620s, by which time firearms and Native mastery of European vessels were becoming widespread. With this, the northerners lost their military advantage.

Trouble with the British

At the same time that these events took place, other pressures were building against indigenous coastal people. In 1605, George Waymouth for Britain and Samuel de Champlain for France entered Penobscot Bay, followed by others of the same nationalities within a few years. The contrast between Champlain and Waymouth in their dealings with the locals is instructive; Champlain visited Bashabas at his headquarters upriver, traded with him, and got along well by all accounts. Waymouth, on the other hand, treated the Indians with arrogance, several times rebuffing invitations from emissaries of Bashabas to visit and trade. From the Indian standpoint, this did not bode well; for to them, trade was as much a diplomatic as an economic activity. In their eyes, failure to trade signaled an unwillingness to engage in diplomacy; an ominous sign. Confirming their anxieties, Waymouth and his crew kidnapped five Indians from the Georges Islands, at the western entrance of Penobscot Bay, taking them back to England.

These encounters of 1605 set the pattern for relations between the Indians, French, and British. With the former, they got along well; with the latter they did not. Two years after Waymouth's voyage, the British tried to establish a colony at the mouth of the Kennebec, where again they managed to antagonize the locals with their arrogant behavior. As one French source reported,

"They [the British] drove the savages away without ceremony; they beat, maltreated, and misused them outrageously." Word of such behavior surely would have spread widely. Bad behavior on the part of the British continued when, in 1611, Captain Edward Harlow kidnapped three Indians on Monhegan Island. Although one escaped, the other two (with five others captured on Cape Cod) were transported to England. By contrast, in the same year a trading party of Frenchmen had an entirely friendly meeting with a large group of Etchemins near the mouth of the Bagaduce River.

Kidnappings by the British continued in 1614 when Thomas Hunt, an associate of John Smith, seized several Indians on Monhegan Island who, with others captured elsewhere, were sold to Spanish slave traders. Things heated up more when the British destroyed the French settlement at St. Sauveur on Mount Desert Island. Established in 1613, the French had been welcomed ashore as friends by the local Indians and their chief, Asticou. From this time on through the 17th, and much of the 18th century, the Penobscot region was contested territory between the French and British, with the Indians looking out for their own interests. Continued friendly relations with the French were promoted by the hostility of both to a common enemy (the British); the French practice of interacting with the Natives on a more or less equal footing, even to the extent of intermarriage; and the openness of trade between the two people. This included the trade (and servicing) of firearms, an act of special significance in Native eyes, for in traditional Indian diplomacy, weapons exchange was a required sign that the parties would deal with one another in good faith. By contrast, the British tried to prevent the trade of firearms to Indians, which the latter only could take as a sign of hostile intent. Strengthening this perception, the British persisted in treating the Natives with contempt, considering them to be no better than wild beasts. To top it all off, following their settlement in southern New England, the British developed an alliance with the Iroquois nations of New York, traditional enemies of the eastern Indians.

With the establishment of the Plymouth and Massachusetts Bay colonies in the 1620s, pressures on the Etchemins' southern neighbors became more and more intense. From the very beginning, the colonists wanted the Indians off the land, and as their numbers grew through a flood of immigration, life for the Natives became increasingly intolerable. As for the Etchemins, their numbers continued to be devastated by repeated outbreaks of European diseases as well as by periodic acts of violence committed by the British and, after 1640, Mohawk raiders. Their response was to fall back on a traditional means of offsetting losses from warfare or natural disasters: adoption of outsiders. In this case, they replenished their numbers by encouraging their Abenaki compatriots from the old Mawooshen Confederacy to find refuge with them in the Penobscot region. Following the outbreak of all-out warfare between Indians and the ever-expanding New England colonies in 1675—a conflict that continued more or less continuously for the next 85 years—the trickle of Abenaki refugees grew to a flood, especially after the 1724 destruction of Norridgewock on the Kennebec River. The end result was that the Abenakis came to outnumber the local Etchemins, and their language came to replace the original one in Penobscot country. Only among the eastern Etchemin did the old language survive, represented today by Passamaquoddy and Maliseet.

Deer Isle and Interaction with Europeans

Although we have few specifics, it is clear that Indians in and around Deer Isle were caught up in all this turmoil. Here, a major canoe route ran through the center of the island (figure 2), connecting the islands to the south with a traditional gathering area for Indians just in from the Castine Peninsula. Feeding into this route from the south through Webb's Cove or Southeast Harbor, or from the east via Greenlaw Cove, travelers proceeded through Long Cove to the Haulover. After a short carry, the route continued through Northwest Harbor, up the coast to the opening between Deer Isle and Little Deer, and across the Reach to the Punch Bowl. Here, an important carry gave access to Walker's Pond and from it, the Bagaduce River. This Meniwoken, or "many directions route" (figure 3) allowed travelers to proceed all the way to the Penobscot

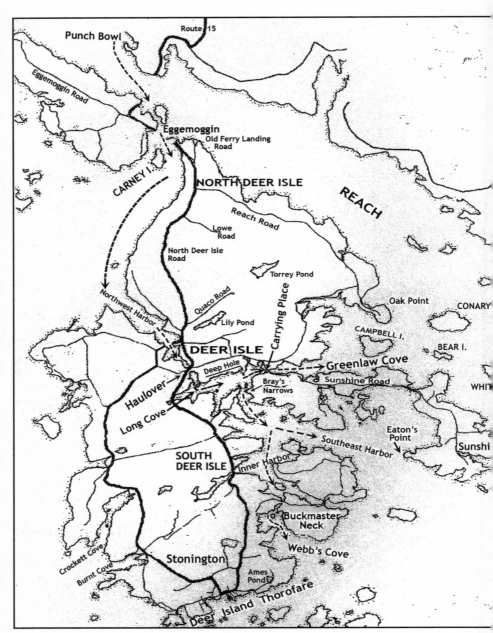

Figure 2. THE DEER ISLE CANOE ROUTE CONNECTED WITH THE MINNEWOKUN ROU(FIGURE 3) AT THE PUNCH BOWL. IT RAN FROM THERE BETWEEN DEER ISLE AND LITDEER, THEN ALONG THE SHORE TO NORTHWEST HARBOR, WITH A CARRY TO LONG CoFROM HERE ONE COULD GO EAST WITH A SHORT CARRY TO GREENLAW COVE, OR SOU

River. Established between 2000 and 3000 years ago, the route was still in use by Indians as recently as the 1920s. Its great advantage was that it offered protection from the winds and other hazards of coastal canoeing, with the added benefit that it ran through country rich in resources of both land and sea. For example, well into the 20th century brooks running into Long Cove were known for their large runs of smelt and tomcod. Flounder spearing, too, was excellent at several spots, and weirs were constructed in the natural fish passage between Deer Isle and Little Deer. And still today, the extensive clam-flats all along the canoe route remain important. An added bonus by 1600 was that by using this route, one could avoid being seen by Mi'kmaq raiders or other hostile vessels cruising in coastal waters.

It is reasonable to suppose that people traveled this route from Deer Isle in 1611 to the mouth of the Bagaduce, where 300 Etchemins in 80 canoes and a shallop met with a French trading party and the Jesuit missionary Pierre Biard. More specific evidence of trade comes from a site along the canoe route on the Mountainville shore of Southeast Harbor (figure 2). Here was found, in 2002, a jetton, a 17th-century accountant's token. About the size of a modern nickel, jettons were used as aids in mathematical calculations. The one found at the Deer Isle site was made in Nuremberg, Germany, and was perforated to be worn as an ornament.

Further evidence of interaction between Indians and Europeans in the early 17th century comes from another site on the canoe route, this one on Campbell's Island, in the mouth of Greenlaw Cove (see figure 2 for location). Discovered in the last years of the 19th century was a burial, including a European in full armor, along with a Native companion. With the European was the iron blade of a halberd, an iron hatchet marked with a Maltese cross, a spike (likely a poignard blade) and the muzzle of a blunderbuss that had been destroyed by pounding it with heavy rocks. With the Native companion were beads, the remains of an iron knife,

THROUGH BRAY'S NARROWS TO SOUTHEAST HARBOR. CONTINUING SOUTH, A SHORT CARRY GAVE ACCESS TO WEBB'S COVE AND THE ISLANDS SOUTH OF STONINGTON. Map by Rodney Chadbourne.

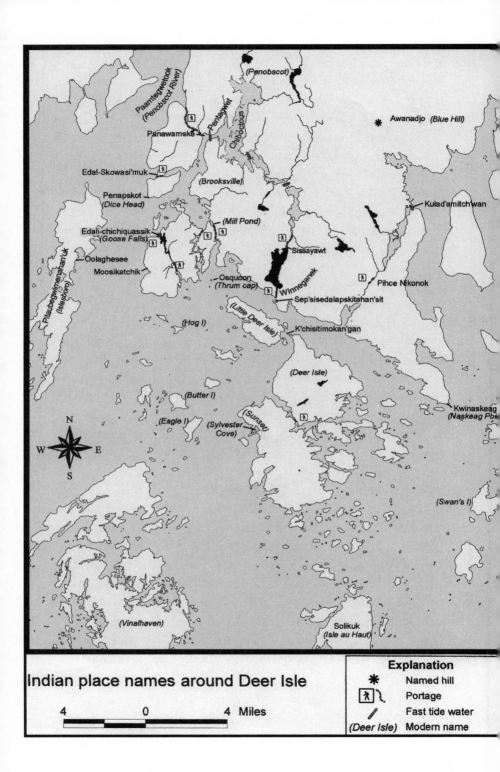

Indian place names around Deer Isle

4   0   4 Miles

Explanation

* — Named hill
[portage symbol] — Portage
/ — Fast tide water
(Deer Isle) — Modern name

Map labels:

(Penobscot)
Paamtegwetook *(Penobscot River)*
Panawamske
Pentagwet
Chiboctous
Awanadjo *(Blue Hill)*
Edal-Skowasi'muk
(Brooksville)
Penapskot *(Dice Head)*
Kulad'amitch'wan
(Mill Pond)
Edali-chichiquassik *(Goose Falls)*
Sissayawt
Oolaghesee
Moosikatchik
Osquoon *(Thrum cap)*
Winneganek
Pihce Nikonok
Sep'sisedalapskitahan'sit
(Little Deer Isle)
Pitaubegwimenahan'uk *(Islesboro)*
(Hog I)
K'chisitimokan'gan
(Deer Isle)
(Butter I)
Kwinaskeag *(Naskeag Point)*
(Eagle I)
(Sunsey)
(Sylvester Cove)
(Swan's I)
(Vinalhaven)
Solikuk *(Isle au Haut)*

MEANINGS OF INDIAN PLACE NAMES AROUND DEER ISLE

Awanadjo	small hazy mountain
Chiboctus	the big bay
Edali-chichiquassik	where there is a very narrow place
Edal-Skowasi'muk	where you must wait
K'chisitimokan'gan	the great fish weir
Kulad'amitch'wan	mixed rapids
Kwinaskeag	the long point
Moosikatchik	the moose's rump
Oolaghesee	the entrail
Osquoon	the moose liver
Paamtegwetook	the main river
Panawamské	opening out upon a ledgy place
Penapskot	at the descending rock
Pentagwet	falls of the river
Pihce Nikonok	long portage
Pitaubegwimenahanuk	the island between two channels
Sep'sisedalapskitahan'sit	where the bird is punched in the rock (petroglyph)
Sissayawt	many directions portage
Solikuk	place of the [empty] shells
Winneganek	the carrying place

Figure 3. EAST PENOBSCOT BAY, WITH INDIAN PLACE NAMES. THE MIN-NEWOKUN CANOE ROUTE FOLLOWED THE BAGADUCE (CALLED CHIBOCTOUS BY THE ETCHEMINS) FROM THE CASTINE PENINSULA TO WALKER'S POND, FROM WHICH A HALF-MILE PORTAGE TOOK ONE TO THE PUNCH BOWL. OTH-ER ROUTES SHOWN HERE ARE THOSE ACROSS CAPE ROSIER: GOOSE POND TO WEIR COVE AND SMITH COVE TO HORSESHOE COVE, AND SMITH COVE TO ORCUTT'S HARBOR, VIA THE "MILL POND." ALSO SHOWN ARE INDIAN PLACE NAMES. Map by Roger and Ann Hooke, place names from Eckstorm (1941) and Soctomah (2004).

several implements of stone, bone and beaver teeth (the latter the antecedents of the crooked knives used historically and even today among Maine's Native people). We do not know whether this individual was a man or woman; if the former, he was clearly a close companion, but if the latter, she may have been the European's wife or partner.

Within three feet of these two individuals was a third, buried in a traditional Indian manner with mineral paint and a few items of European manufacture. The remains seem to reflect friendly relationships between all three individuals. All had been respectfully laid to rest, the flattened blunderbuss being the result of the traditional Indian practice of ritually "killing" an object placed with the deceased, thereby releasing its animating spirit. Most likely, the European was associated with Pentagoet, the French outpost where Castine is today. Here, the French had a presence as early as 1615.

A Casualty of War on Deer Isle

Another apparent burial, this one somewhere on Deer Isle, may also date from the early 1600s. Sometime around 1825, a large hardwood tree blew over, exposing beneath its roots two relatively complete human skeletons. One was described at the time as being that of someone "at least eight feet tall," the other from a person of "ordinary size." Clearly, one individual was larger and more robust than the other, although the size of the larger likely is overstated. Probably, the one was a male; less certainty, the other was a female.

Lodged between the ribs of the probable man was an arrow point made of copper. As already noted, among the items obtained by Indians in their trade with Europeans were copper kettles, some of which were broken into pieces to make arrow points. Such may have been the origin of this one. A likely scenario is that this man and his companion met their end in the course of a Mi'kmaq raid.

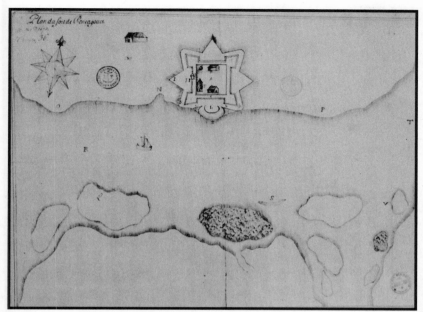

Figure 4. A 1670 FRENCH PLAN OF THEIR FORT PENTAGOET AT THE MOUTH OF THE BAGADUCE. From Faulkner and Faulkner 1987:55.

The Battle of Walker's Pond

Although Plymouth colonists in 1626 established a trading post somewhere on the bay or river, French control of the Penobscot region was recognized by treaty in 1632. Despite occasional raids by the British, the French remained in control, from their fort at Pentagoet (figure 4) until driven out in 1654. With the British then installed at Fort Pentagoet, where they remained until 1670, things could not have been happy for the Indians. To them, English-speaking foreigners were unwelcome invaders of their country, nor could they rely on them for such useful services as the French had provided, such as gunsmithing and supplies of powder and shot. It was during this period of British occupation that a major incident took place just across the Reach from Deer Isle.

Sometime around 1660, Indians seized a fishing vessel in the Punch Bowl, which they burned, killing the crew as well. The Indians came from a village on the north shore of Walker's Pond,

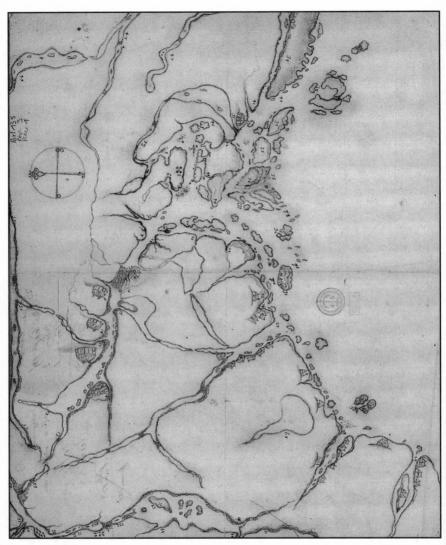

Figure 5. 1671 MAP OF THE PENOBSCOT DRAINAGE PREPARED BY THE CHEVALIER
DE GRANDFONTAINE, GOVERNOR OF ACADIA. NORTH IS LEFT, 37 AND 35 ARE
DEER ISLE (CALLED THE FOUNDRY ISLANDS) AND LITTLE DEER RESPECTIVELY;
ACROSS THE REACH IS SHOWN AN INDIAN FORT. ALTHOUGH IT MIGHT APPEAR
TO BE LOCATED ON BYARD'S POINT, THIS IS UNLIKELY, AS ITS PROXIMITY TO THE
REACH WOULD MAKE IT VULNERABLE TO ENEMY RAIDERS. SUCH FORTS WERE
PLACES OF REFUGE AND WERE LIKELY TO BE BACK FROM PLACES OF IMMEDIATE
DANGER. Document conservé aux Archives Nationales, Paris. Cliché Atelier
Photographique des Archives Nationales.

a short distance west of its outlet into the Bagaduce River. Just when the village was established we do not know, but its existence by late in the 16th century is certain. Sometime between 1580 and 1600, its residents laid to rest two children who had died, probably from one of the diseases that accompanied Europeans to North America.

To the British, the vessel's destruction was one of a number of depredations committed by Indians around and in the Reach. The Indians, however, were concerned with defending their homeland and its resources in the face of a foreign occupation. Moreover, knowing what we do of the generally provocative behavior of the British toward Indians, and of the importance in Native culture of avenging injuries committed against them, it is likely that they were taking vengeance for some previous British misdeed. What that may have been we do not know.

The British, in turn, retaliated for the loss of their vessel and crew by launching a surprise raid on the village. The surviving account has it that the village was attacked at dawn and burned, and all its inhabitants killed, save one who escaped. There is, however, reason to believe that the victory was not as total as claimed. A 1671 map (figure 5), commissioned by the governor at Fort Pentagoet following French resumption of control, shows an Indian fort, apparently at the head of Walker's Pond. Probably, the village was relocated to this spot. Moreover, we have reports a century later of an Indian village "not far from Herricks." We know, too, that the British raiders were led by a Native guide, who was acting under duress, and who took several hours longer to reach the village than necessary. This would have allowed time for word of the impending attack to be gotten to the villagers, enabling them to make good their escape. This is not unlike other instances where Indians are known to have evacuated villages about to be attacked, owing to advanced warnings from sympathetic scouts.

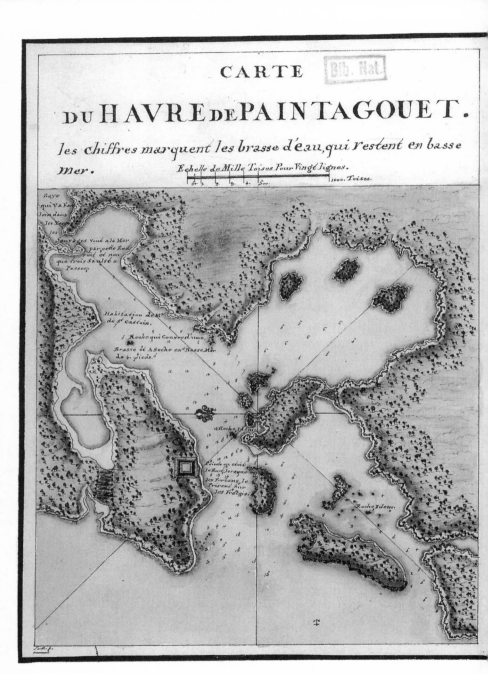

CARTE

DU HAVRE DE PAINTAGOUET.

les chiffres marquent les brasse d'eau, qui restent en basse mer.

Echelle de Mille Toises Pour Vingt lignes.

1000. Toises.

Baye qui Va Fort Join dans les Bois

les Sauvages Vont a la Mer par cette End
ront et non que trois Saults a
Passer

Habitation de Mr
de St Castin.

Roche qui Couvre d'une.
Brasse ét A Seche en Basse Mer
de 4. pieds.

Roche Idem.

Roche Idem.

Pointe ou étoit
le Fort Jorgine
et Jouiant. le
les Fontans. Je
Trouvent Sur
les Frotigus

Roche Idem.

Figure 6. This 1688 map of Pentagoet Harbor shows Saint-Castin's habitation on the point across Hatch Cove from the Castine Peninsula. Unlike the for it was closer to the locality favored by the Indians for their encampment FR. ANOM. Aix-en-Provence (Cote du document). Tous droits réservés.

The End of the Century and the Wabanaki Confederacy

For the rest of the 17th century we have no specific evidence for human activity, Indian or otherwise, on Deer Isle or in its immediate neighborhood. People must have been here, for they were all around the area, and there was a great deal of activity going on. To cite a few examples, the 1667 treaty of Breda returned the region east of Pemaquid to the French, even though the British governor stalled for three years before turning over Fort Pentagoet. In 1674, Dutch raiders dismantled and burned the fort, but their success was short-lived. In 1675 William Waldron kidnapped fifteen Indians near Machias, whom he sold into slavery in the Azores, an act that so outraged the Natives as to trigger all-out warfare with the British. A year later the regional chief (and father-in-law of Baron de Saint-Castin), Madockawando, agreed to peace, and in 1677 Saint-Castin restored French authority at Pentagoet. But peace remained elusive; by the 1680s there were further outbreaks of fighting, and in 1688 New England's Governor Andros pillaged Saint-Castin's trading post (figure 6). On the other side, many a raid against settlements in southern Maine were launched from the Penobscot region. This prompted the Massachusetts Bay Colony in 1697 to send a punitive expedition into the area. Among the places where this force sought French and Indian enemies was Naskeag, where they found "several Housing and small Fields of Corn," but the people were gone. This mention of corn is of interest, for it is indicative of the presence of Abenakis. With a tradition of corn cultivation, refugees brought this practice with them when they came to live among the Etchemins, who were not farmers.

By the end of the 17th century, the reaction of the Indians along the coast to seemingly incessant conflict was to create an alliance between Abenakis, Etchemins, and their one-time enemies the Mi'kmaqs. Representing a rebirth of the old Mawooshen Confederacy, but on a larger scale, this new one came to be known as the Wabanaki (Dawnland) Confederacy.

II

The Eighteenth Century

For this century, we have no specific reference to Native activities until the end of the French and Indian Wars, in 1760. But as before, much was going on in the vicinity. Moreover, in February, 1723, British scouts ranging along the coast from the Kennebec to Mount Desert Island, and who we know put into Burnt Coat Harbor on Swan's Island, from where they sailed up the Reach and on up the Penobscot River, observed that they "met . . . numbers of wigwams on almost every island and the mainland, where we have rang'd, which we judge were deserted in the fall." Surely, some of those wigwams were seen on Deer Isle and/or Little Deer.

Adventures of the Castin Children

As for specific incidents happening in the vicinity, many involved the sons and daughters of the Baron de Saint-Castin (he having departed for France in 1701 to regain his ancestral home there). In 1703 at Naskeag, the English privateer Samuel Chadwell raided the home of Philippe Meunier and his wife Brigitte d'Abbadie, one of the daughters of Saint-Castin and his Indian wife Molly Matilde. Married just that year, Meunier was killed and his wife raped, and perhaps killed. This so outraged the Indians that they raided Casco and Wells, prompting Massachusetts to declare war on the Indians. One year into that war Brigitte's older sister Claire, with her children, was captured somewhere on the bay and held a prisoner in Boston, probably till the war's end in 1713. Thereafter, she went to live on Mount Desert Island.

A brother of Claire and Brigitte was Bernard-Anselm d'Abbadie de Saint-Castin (he inherited his father's title). In 1710, on a trip east from Penobscot Bay, his ketch was captured by the English, but he managed to escape. Later that year we find him guiding a British envoy from Port Royal, Nova Scotia, recently captured by the English, to Quebec, to see the French governor. The route they took passed from Blue Hill Bay to the Penobscot River via Pentagoet; most likely, the party traveled through Salt Pond and the Benjamin River (via the Pihce Nikonok carry; see figure 3), then up the Reach to the Punch Bowl, and from there to Walker's Pond and down the Bagaduce. A year later, Bernard was acting as a guerilla leader against the English around Port Royal.

A 1713 treaty ushered in an uneasy period of peace and explicitly acknowledged the aboriginal rights of the Indians, even while asserting English dominion over what had been French Acadia. Nevertheless, the situation deteriorated, as developers cast covetous eyes on land east of Pemaquid, and fishermen increasingly interfered with traditional subsistence pursuits along the coast. Then, in 1721, the English kidnapped Joseph d'Abbadie (a brother of Bernard) who, with a younger brother, Barenos, operated a fur trading business. In mid-June of the same year, local Indians—perhaps relatives of Joseph and Barenos—captured some Massachusetts fishermen probably in Fox Island Thorofare. In 1722, a New England sloop that put into the harbor at Pentagoet was seized by a party of eighty Indians, and by 1723, full-scale warfare had returned. With this, Massachusetts posted bounties of up to £200 for Indian scalps. Although the British did not invent scalping, what they did do was turn it into a commercial operation.

There is a story that one of the captives taken in this new conflict was Ruth, the mother of Meribah Wardwell. In 1742, in York, Meribah married William Eaton, who would become one of Deer Isle's earliest English-speaking settlers 20 years later. As the story goes, Ruth Wardwell was captured in an Abenaki raid in southern Maine and, while in captivity, conceived and gave birth to her daughter. In fact, Meribah was born in York in 1720, nor was her mother taken captive. Ruth did have a cousin, sister-in-law and half-sister who were captured, just before and after 1700.

Evidently, a confusion of identities over the years gave rise to the story of Meribah's birth.

Incidents near Deer Isle during the war included capture of a Marblehead schooner fishing near North Haven or Vinalhaven by Joseph d'Abbadie and several Indians in June of 1724. The same year saw the capture of eight more vessels and the killing of their crews in the same general area. The Indians evidently made good use of the vessels they captured, for in 1725, authorities in Massachusetts complained that Indians "now infest the eastern coast in a schooner [actually, more than one] by them taken from the English."

Another episode occurred in the summer of 1725 when one of the Saint-Castin brothers anchored a sloop in Naskeag harbor. What happened next is described by Roger Duncan in his book on coastal Maine:

> With him was his young son and Samuel Trask, a Salem boy whom Castin had ransomed. An "English" sloop, probably a colonial vessel, came up Jericho Bay, saw an Indian and two boys aboard, and fired on Castin. Castin and the boys fled ashore. The skipper of the sloop raised a white flag, hailed Castin, said the shooting was a "mistake," and invited him aboard. The skipper then seized Trask and declared that Castin and his son were his prisoners. All hands went ashore. When one of the sloop's crew seized the Indian boy, evidently with the intention of taking him away from his father, Castin shot the man dead and with his son disappeared into the forest. Clearly, there was no military value to be gained. But Indian scalps and Indian captives were worth hard money in Boston.

By the fall, the Penobscots (as the surviving Mawooshen population of Etchemins and Abenaki refugees was now called) agreed to lay down their arms, in return for which a sloop was sent from Boston to "Agemogen" (Eggemoggin) with trade goods as well as hostages to be returned to the Indians. The sloop arrived at the designated place—the passage between Deer Isle and Little

Figure 7. THIS CLAY PIPE WAS FOUND ON A BEACH IN THE VICINITY OF "AGEMO-GEN." PROBABLY MADE IN SCOTLAND, IT DATES FROM AROUND THE TIME OF THE 1726 VISIT OF THE BOSTON SLOOP AND MAY HAVE BEEN LOST BY A MEMBER OF HER CREW. Photo by author.

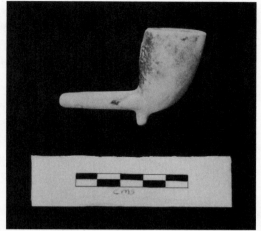

Deer—in January, by which time the Indians had removed to Mount Desert, and the vessel got frozen in the ice. Nevertheless, the parties did connect and the exchanges took place.

The choice of Agemogen for the rendezvous may reflect its importance as a meeting place for Indians. Testing an archaeological site here in 2003, Steve Cox of the Maine State Museum recovered, along with Indian pottery and tools of bone and stone, a small blue glass bead, Kaolin pipe stems, a thin sherd of glass, and redware sherds (all historic material). This suggests that, although they missed each other here in 1726, Indians and "whites" did meet at this location on other occasions.

Trouble at Matinicus

All these decades of conflict, not to mention periodic outbreaks of diseases of European origin, lethal to Indians, took a heavy toll. Nonetheless, as of 1726, an official tally of Indians living east of Boston listed the Penobscots as having 90 warriors, which would imply a total population on the order of 450. In the brief interval of peace before the next conflict, these people went about their traditional pursuits, not always without friction with the British. For example, in February of 1727, a group of twelve Penobscots traveled to Matinicus to hunt seals (a traditional point of departure for such a trip was Isle Au Haut). Unfortunately for them, they found no seals, and to make matters worse, the weather turned bad and they were marooned for several days. To survive, they killed a cow and a hog they found on the island, at which the colonists expressed outrage.

This was not the first instance of conflicting interests on Matinicus, nor was it the last. As early as 1686, Massachusetts authorities warned Saint-Castin not to threaten English fishermen on the island. Later, in 1755 the Penobscots made a formal complaint about English seal hunters interfering with their own hunting and fowling. As the Penobscot chief put it: "God hath planted us here, God gave us this land: and we will keep it. God decreed all things; he decreed this land to us; therefore neither shall the French or English possess it, but we will."

In 1757, a more serious incident occurred on the island. In that year Ebenezer Hall, who was then living on Matinicus, was murdered, and his family abducted. Besides fishing, Hall was in the business of selling hay in Boston, and to promote its growth, he regularly burned over Green Island. But for the Indians, this island was important as a source of eggs and seabirds for meat. Although they successfully petitioned the Massachusetts authority to get Hall to stop, there was no enforcement, and Hall persisted in burning over the island. For the Indians, it was one more example of English deceit, and so they took matters into their own hands.

The Final Conflict

So the hostilities continued, with open warfare erupting between 1743 and 1748. Although the treaty that ended the previous war was reinstated, real peace remained illusory. A final conflict erupted in 1754, although the Penobscots tried hard to remain neutral, even in the face of considerable provocation, such as that just noted in the case of Matinicus. But it was not to be; although they assured the British they would not take up arms against them, when the Indians refused to fight those Abenakis who had taken up arms, they were officially declared "enemies, rebels and traitors to his

PROCLAMATION

GIVEN at the Council Chamber of the Great and General Court of the Province of Massachusetts in Boston this third day of November 1755.

Whereas the tribe of Penobscot Indians have repeatedly in a perfidious manner acted contrary to their solemn submission unto his Majesty long since made and frequently renewed,

I have, therefore, at the desire of the House of Representatives, thought fit to issue this Proclamation and to declare the Penobscot Tribe of Indians to be enemies, rebels and traitors to his Majesty. And I do hereby require his Majesty's subjects of the Province to embrace all opportunities of pursuing, captivating, killing and destroying all and every of the aforesaid Indians.

And whereas the General Court of this Province have voted that a bounty be granted and allowed to be paid out of the Province Treasury, the premiums of bounty following, viz.:

For every scalp of a male Indian brought in as evidence of their being killed as aforesaid, forty pounds.

For every scalp of such female Indian or male Indian under the age of twelve years that shall be killed and brought in as evidence of their being killed as aforesaid, twenty pounds.

By his Honour's command

J. Willard, Secry.

God Save the King

Figure 8. THE PROCLAMATION OF 1755 SETTING A BOUNTY ON PENOBSCOT INDIAN SCALPS. From Speck (1997:XIX–XX).

most sacred majesty." With this, Massachusetts pledged to pay a bounty of £40 for every scalp of a male Indian, or £20 for those of females or males under 12 years of age (figure 8). Later, the bounty was raised to £300. For the Indians, this meant that to be seen was to be marked for death. As if this were not bad enough, yet another epidemic swept through Native populations; in this case, smallpox. As a consequence, they were too debilitated to do much fighting. Still, incidents occurred, such as the murder of Ebenezer Hall already noted. Another incident took place at nearby Naskeag. Here, on a summer day in 1758, a party of eleven British bounty hunters in a sloop spotted a group of Indians. Unfortunately for them, the hunters soon found themselves drawn into an ambush by about forty canoes.

A year later Governor Thomas Pownall was moved to observe that "the Penobscot Country . . . [was] a Den for Savages and a lurking place for some Renegadoe French [with] Indianized Frenchmen intermixed with them." Thus, he proposed to build a fort [Fort Pownall] at the mouth of the river, to close "the last and only door that the enemy had left to the Atlantic."

Figure 9. FORT POWNALL WAS BUILT AT THE MOUTH OF THE PENOBSCOT RIVER IN 1759, IN ORDER TO BLOCK INDIAN ACCESS TO THE COAST. THE FORT'S REMAINS CAN BE SEEN TODAY, JUST IN FROM FORT POINT LIGHTHOUSE. Photo by author.

Indians and Deer Isle's First British Settlers

With the fall of Montreal in 1760, formalized by the Treaty of Paris in 1763, the last of the French and Indian Wars came to an end, and a rush of English settlers into the region began. Yet, it is clear that significant numbers of Indians remained in the region. In 1763, Governor Francis Bernard (who succeeded Pownall) proclaimed that English colonists were not allowed to settle east of the Penobscot River. However, a rather large exception was made to grant him Mount Desert Island. Otherwise, Indians were not to be disturbed Downeast. But disturbed they were, by early settlers from Deer Isle among others, as the following petition attests.

INDIAN PETITION

To the honourable Council and House of Representatives of the Massachusetts-Bay:

We, the petitioners, humble showeth, we being inhabitants to the Province of Massachusetts-Bay, and friends to the United States of America, did on the 25th day of October, set out on our hunting business, in order to support ourself and family, on the branches of Union river, where we use to hunt for our support. At our arrival at the branches we found all the hunting grounds taken up by Englishmen from Deer-Island and Bagaduse, which is great disappointment to us; having no other way to support ourself and family, we beg your Honours would take our circumstances into consideration, and do something to prevent the Englishmen from hunting, or we and our family will suffer, as we are afraid to go back in the limits of Canada as we use to do.

Gentlemen, your attentions to the above will oblige your friend and humble servant,

his
JOSEPH X PLOARQUA
mark

his
ACTON X NOCKTUMBARURAR
mark

his
JOSEPH X RORAN
mark

his
SER X CARTIS
mark

Witness:
John Ray
Joseph Jewett
Union River, November 2, 1776

One of the earliest Anglo settlers on Deer Isle is said to be William Greenlaw, who came with his family from Warren, perhaps as early as 1760. By then, a de facto peace had settled in, and other English-speaking settlers began to arrive on Deer Isle. The earliest to stay consisted of William Eaton with his wife Meribah and their children. The Eatons settled on the very northern end of Deer Isle, where the ferry landing and steamboat wharf were later established. Included in their land was the old Agemogen, site of the 1726 meeting between Indians and colonists. According to Vera Powers Billings:

My grandmother Lucinda (Gray) Powers told my mother about the Indians who were living at the northern end of the island near the Little Deer Isle bar. Major William Eaton had a bull which the Indians were much afraid of. They called it "All One Devil" and because of it moved away from that part of the island.

Although George Hosmer, in his *Historical Sketch of the Town of Deer Isle*, made no mention of Indians living here at the time, he did note "when the land was plowed, the spots upon which they had built their wigwams were easily discernible." Because "it was the work of years to clear the land for the plow," these wigwams may have been abandoned some time prior to the 1760s. Perhaps they were the ones seen "on almost every island" by those British scouts in 1723. Nevertheless, in the 1760s, some Indians were living on the island, and we can be sure that they continued to use the old Deer Isle canoe route, since they were still doing so well into the 20th century.

Another early Anglo settler of Deer Isle was Seth Webb, who arrived in 1765. According to Hosmer, he

> took up a lot near what is now known as Webb's Cove [on the canoe route]; he also, a part of the time, resided upon Kimball's Island, now in the town of Isle Au Haut, and was there during the war of the Revolution. When he left Windham [Maine], he owned considerable property, but having a fondness for hunting, he came East, and was during much of his time engaged in that pursuit with the Indians, with whom he was on good terms, and frequently those with whom he associated, made his house their home when about here. Among others who did so was a noted man among them, a chief named Orono, reputed to be a natural son of one of the sons of the Baron de Castine. Orono lived to a very great age, and was said to be one hundred and ten years old at the time of his death. I have often heard Mr. Webb's last surviving daughter speak of his being at her father's house frequently. Mr. Webb hunted much upon Union River and its tributaries, and in all probability, the pond near it, now known as Webb's Pond, and the brook leading out of it were named for him.

Webb's reported friendship with Indians is of interest, in that he had been captured by them and then ransomed in 1752, just before the last of the Indian Wars. The cellar hole of his house can

Figure 10. THIS VIEW FROM THE EAST SIDE OF WEBB'S COVE SHOWS THE POINT OF LAND WHERE SETH WEBB SETTLED AND PLAYED HOST TO PENOBSCOT CHIEF ORONO. Photo by author.

still be seen near the shore of Webb's cove, a major transportation route, not far from productive clam-flats and the outlet of a brook from Burntland Pond that, historically, saw large annual eel runs. Also nearby were productive smelt brooks. The combination would have made the place exceedingly attractive to Indians, so Webb was well positioned for interaction with them. On the other hand, could it be that he was one of those "Englishmen from Deer Island" hunting on the Union River who were the subject of the earlier mentioned complaint of 1776?

The Orono referred to in Hosmer's account was Joseph Orono, the Penobscot's head chief whose animal emblem was the beaver, and who died in 1801. According to his son-in-law, he was related to "Old Castine"; evidently the son of one of the Baron's daughters and grandson of the Etchemin chief Madockawando. Orono was a tall, thin man with a pale complexion, blue eyes and reddish hair. He was devoted to the French, and spoke their language, as well as his own. His nickname was K'tolaqu, meaning "frigate." This was because he talked so much about French warships he had visited in 1780 when in Newport, Rhode Island, on a mission to request a priest from the French consul there.

With an eye to the future, he led a Penobscot delegation to meet with the Provincial Congress of Massachusetts at Watertown at the onset of the American Revolution. There, they agreed to come in on the side of the rebels in return for rights to six miles of land on each side of their river above the head of tide. True to their promise, Penobscots fought at Castine in 1779 and after the American defeat there, met with authorities at Treat's Truck House near Bangor and, in defiance of Mohawk threats, pledged to stand with the colonists. Orono himself served the cause by carrying messages for the Americans to Machias, the Saint John River and Halifax. But true to form, Massachusetts reneged on their part of the bargain and, in 1796, forced Orono into signing a treaty to quit most of their land on the river. This was subsequently divided into nine townships.

After the Revolution, Orono and his followers were frequently spotted on islands east of Sunshine, and one island off Swan's is even named for him. Following a split among the Penobscots shortly after 1783, he and a group of Catholic followers went with a Recollet Missionary and established a headquarters on White Island, with several wigwams and a chapel. At a meeting there in 1786, with Massachusetts Commissioner Benjamin Lincoln, he complained bitterly about attempts by white settlers to evict him and his companions. It seems that, a year earlier, Thomas Stinson (in spite of a dubious title) sold the island to Benjamin York, who proceeded to cut wood on the island, and to burn the Indians' dwellings and chapel.

Indians living near Deer Isle included some encountered by John Billings when he moved across the Reach from Little Deer in 1767. According to Chatto and Turner, in their 1910 *Register*, he built "his log cabin near an Indian village not far from Herricks within the limits of what is now Brooksville. Here he lived at peace with the Indians for many years, and his children played with the Indian children." Local histories of Brooksville place Billings' cabin on the west shore of Walker's Pond, near its south end. The village referred to could well be the successor to the one attacked by the British in the 1660s. At the north end of the pond, the village's original location, "white" settlers in John Billings' time dug bullets out of the pine trees. And in 1910, according to Chatto and Turner, "Not far from the [Oakland House], Herricks . . . may be seen still a few plants and herbs alien to the soil, marking the location of an ancient Indian garden."

A story about a hunter on Carney Island, where the Deer Isle canoe route passes after emerging from the passage between Little Deer and the main island pertains to the early days of Anglo settlement; how much of it is true and how much is made up is not known. It does reflect the hostility toward the Natives still held by some after the long period of conflict. Known only through oral tradition, the story goes like this: a "white" hunter was stalking his prey on Carney Island when, behind him, he heard a "click." It was the misfiring of a flintlock musket; the hunter himself was being stalked by an Indian who tried to shoot him, but the shot failed to go off. Thus, the hunter was able to turn the tables and shoot the Indian.

The Story of Conary Island

Several versions of a story exist about the murder in 1789 or soon after of an Indian on Conary Island, just off the Greenlaw Cove branch of the Deer Isle canoe route (figure 2). In a 1786 treaty, Massachusetts proposed to reserve Conary (then called Black Island), White, and Waukeag islands for the Indians in return for the surrender of aboriginal claims along the Penobscot River (the present-day identity of Waukeag Island is not known). So it was that when Thomas Conary purchased the island in 1789, an Indian named Swunksus was already living there. There are several versions of what happened next; here is one:

> H. B. Wardwell tells the *Belfast Journal* the following good Indian legend concerning a well-known locality in Maine. At the eastern entrance of Eggemoggin Reach, and within the corporated limits of Deer Isle, is situated Conary Island, containing upward of 200 acres. It was first settled about 1765 [actually 1789] by Mr. Conary. At this time there was an

abundance of wild fruit, and the excellent pasturage made it a fine feeding ground for moose and deer, (etc.) . . . Here Mr. Conary lived in luxurious idleness and plenty. But, alas . . . Strong drink led to frequent quarrels between Conary and Swunksus, the aboriginal proprietor of the land. There was room enough for both, and game and fruit enough for both, but as usual the white man wanted it all, and poor Swunksus wanted a part. So bitter did their quarrel become that one day in Northwest Harbor, by mutual agreement, they parted without a fight, and at their next meeting were to kill each other by fair means if possible . . . They shook hands and parted. Swunksus took a more direct route through the woods, [actually, he would have taken the traditional canoe route from the Haulover through Long Cove and Greenlaw Cove] and having a lighter canoe arrived at the island first and concealed himself near the landing to await the coming of Conary. Then to cheer himself in his weary waiting he took a big drink from his rum jug, and overcome by the potency of the liquor fell into a deep sleep . . .* Conary by this time was returning, and as he cautiously approached the shore heard a loud snoring . . . Silently he landed, and in the dim twilight crept to where the Indian lay in drunken sleep, placed the muzzle of the gun to his ear . . . A shallow grave was dug and all that was mortal of the red man was soon covered from sight. But his shadow still walks the island he loved so well. Sometimes his deep, heavy snoring may be heard in broad sunlight; often is the solitary fisherman or the summer tourist startled by the unearthly sounds as darkness gathers over the deep.

Bearing a startling resemblance to this story's ending is another, dating in this case to the first half of the 20th century. Its protagonist is Greg Merchant, who was a well-known collector of Indian "relics," and the location is a site on the canoe route. And again several versions exist, but the plot remains the same. Here is

*In one version of this story, Conary is the drunk, but the gist of the story—him murdering Swunksus to gain undisputed claim to the island—remains the same.

the version told by Lloyd Capen in his autobiography, *The Price of Clams* (the name he uses is a fictional one):

> Old man Ezekiel Balding dug up three graves at the point at Southeast Harbor finding copper beads and two ceremonial pipes. The next day when he was walking home from Gene Joyce's barber shop at dusk, he heard Indians dancing on the gravel road near his camp. Once inside his camp, his wife told him that Indian spirits had been marching around the log camp all afternoon. Lighting his lantern and carrying his rifle, the old man returned all of the artifacts that he had robbed from a chief's grave. As he neared his cabin, a swirling wind like a dirt devil blew out the lantern light and Ezekiel had to run for it in the dark.

The story of Conary Island did not end with the death of Swunksus. On January 25, 1831, Penobscot Lt. Gov. John Neptune and Joseph SocBasin, delegate, wrote the following to "His excellency Governor Smith":

> There are three islands westerly of Mount Desert, not far from Naskeag Point in Sedgwick called White Island, Black Island and Waukeag Island, which the Indians have always used for landing, stopping and fishing. But lately some white men have come upon the islands, built one house there and say to us they will not let the Indians haul up their canoes there, nor camp, nor do anything in these anymore. We pray that all white people may be told to go away from these three islands, let the Indians use them as their fathers have always done.

Worth noting here is the origin of the Neptune family name among the coastal Indians, which is to say, the Etchemins. As reconstructed by Fannie Eckstorm, in response to the upsets of the 17th and 18th centuries, Neptunes removed from the Penobscot region to Passamaquoddy country where, from at least 1725, there is a string of Neptune chiefs. Some, however, returned to their old homeland, and by 1757 we find a Neptune serving as a Penobscot chief. Like Orono, they are descendants of the earlier regional chief Madockawando, but through one of his daughters married to an Indian man.

III

The Nineteenth Century

In 1888, it was reported that:

> Citizens in Belfast on Penobscot Bay founded the Eggemoggin Tribe, No 11, Improved Order of the Red Men. It was "instituted at Green's Landing [now Stonington] November 15, by Great Sachem A. I. Mather of Belfast." Also elected were a sachem, senior sagamore, junior sagamore, prophet, chief of records, keeper of wampum, first sannup, guard of wigwam, guard of forest, 1st, 2nd, 3rd, and 4th warriors, first powwow, 1st-4th braves, etc. "The tribe is composed of the most prominent businessmen of the place. They have ordered first-class paraphernalia . . . A Council of Pocahontas [for white women] will be organized in about three weeks."

Who were these "Red Men"? According to a 1928 source,

> one of the largest fraternal societies and the oldest and largest strictly American fraternity is the Improved Order of Red Men. First incorporated in 1835 . . . The earlier patriots, who founded the Old Sons of Liberty in Colonial times, never knew what real American liberty was, they having lived under kings all their lives, and having no vote or voice in some of the most important matters pertaining to their own government. Their first vision of real freedom was caught from the wild savages, who roamed the forests at will rejoicing in the unrestrained occupation of this great new world; who selected their own sachems and forms of religious worship;

and who made their own laws and tribal regulations, which were few and simple ... while the white men, who came here, were continually followed up and hampered by unreasonable laws and regulations, imposed by a distant king and his local appointees . . . and were burdened by unjust taxes. They began to chafe under their thralldom, which finally resulted in the "Boston Tea Party," the Declaration of Independence, and the War of the Revolution.

The order was first introduced into the State of Maine by the institution of Squando Tribe, No. 1, at Biddeford, November 6, 1875, this tribe and others instituted prior to 1888 were placed under the jurisdiction of the Great Council of New Hampshire. On October 25, 1888, the Great Council of Maine was instituted in the city of Bath ... At that time there were nine tribes in the Reservation of Maine: Rockmego, No. 2, Auburn; Machigonne, No. 3, Portland; Nahanda, No. 4, Rockland; Cogawesco, No. 5, Portland; Abenakis, No. 6, Bangor; Mecadecut, No. 7, Rockport; Segochet, No. 8, Warren; Pokumkeswawaumokesis, No. 9, Lewiston; Mavooshan, No. 10, Pemaquid. These tribes had a combined membership of 698 . . .

The word "Redmanship" means Americanism. The history of the Improved Order of Red Men is coincident with that of the United States of America. It is a purely pure American organization. To become a member of the Improved Order of Red Men, one must be a *white* American citizen [Italics mine].

The irony here is that the rise of such organizations as the "Red Men," that took their inspiration from Indians, happened in the same century in which it was widely believed that Indians were on the verge of disappearing in the United States. From their earliest encounters, many Europeans were convinced that the original inhabitants of the Americas were destined to disappear, if not physically, then by assimilation, as they gave way to a supposedly superior civilization. The belief gained impetus with the westward expansion of the United States and the attendant Indian wars.

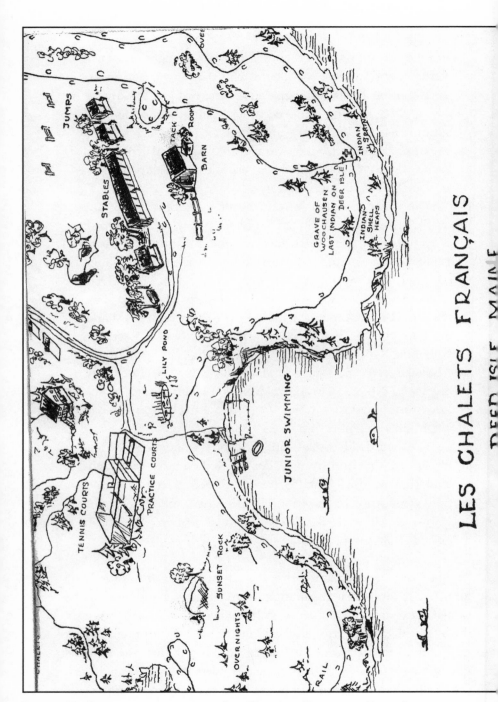

Figure 11. PORTION OF A MAP OF LES CHALETS FRANÇAIS, DEER ISLE, SHOWING THE PURPORTED GRAVE OF THE ISLAND'S SUPPOSED LAST INDIAN.

It achieved expression in the many stories of "last Indians" that became popular in both literature and oral tradition.

The (Untrue) Story of Deer Isle's Last Indian

Not surprisingly, Deer Isle has its own "last Indian" story, and here it is, as told by Clayton Gross in the *Island Ad-Vantages* of August 26, 1999:

> Under a small mound of earth on the southern shore of Les Chalets Français (The French Camp) [figure 11] at Mountainville was buried the last American Indian to have lived on the island. He was buried more than a century and half ago, but the authenticity of the burial spot and many episodes of his life were vouched for by Capt. [Belcher] Howard, former owner of the property, who in turn obtained his information from an old resident. The story had come down to the latter by direct descent.
>
> The Penobscot name of this remarkable Indian was Wouch-ow-sen which translated means "Brave of the Winds," appropriate because of his prowess in sailing and canoeing along the rocky coast. "Legend has it that he was buried on the shore of Deer Isle because he had often expressed the wish that he be buried near a certain large granite rock, extending into the ocean, through a fissure of which, at low tide trickled a stream of pure cold fresh water. At high tide this rock and the spring were completely covered with salt water."
>
> Wouch-ow-sen possessed a strong physique and was capable of performing feats which required unusual strength, agility and intelligence. He was a natural storyteller and held both children and their elders spellbound with his tales of tribal rites and ceremonies, of council fires held on "Council Rock" and of hunters refreshing themselves at "Spring Rock." He tried to impress upon his audience how happy and content the Penobscot people had been on this beautiful island.

Unfortunately, Wouch-ow-sen fell in love with a girl named Elizabeth and encountered racial prejudice. But "the ideal love of these two was never shaken, and they continued to meet each other at various places along the southern shore of what is now known as Mountainville, every spot of which

Figure 12. The "Grave of Wouch-ow-sen," as it appeared in 2003. Photo by author.

was associated with memories." Their story had a tragic ending, when Elizabeth and her father were lost on a fishing trip during a storm. Wouch-ow-sen was heartbroken, and while paddling his canoe on a solitary journey along the shore, was killed by an arrow, either accidentally or deliberately shot from the bow of a member of the Penobscot group visiting the island.

Entertaining though the story may be, there is little (if any) truth to it. The fact is, it tells us more about the attitudes of "whites" than it does about Indians. Gross' source for the story was Dr. George E. Nitzsche, whose daughters owned and operated the French camp. When queried about the story, Nitzsche's grandson, George James, replied to me as follows:

> The legend of Wouch-ow-sen, I am afraid, was a legend promoted by my grandfather. As you might guess, I am named after George Nitzsche. He and I spent a great deal of time together because I was the oldest grandchild and always needed a "male influence" around all of the girls at the camp! There is no question Belcher Howard, the person the family purchased the camp property from around 1935 or 1936, loved to visit with my grandfather and they told tales. The Wouch-ow-sen legend was framed by Belcher and refined by my granddad.
>
> The picture of the gravesite brings back lots of memories. First, I was with my granddad when he decided that the small mound between three small oak saplings, now big trees in the photo, was a likely spot for a grave. I helped him put the cross at that location. The ledge with the spring always fascinated me. The spring did not have cold water because the ledge seemed to warm the water. The flow was very small and the "cup" in the rock was greatly enlarged by my hours of hitting the spot with a hammer. The most convincing thing about the location as far as I was concerned was the "kitchen midden" or shell heap very near the "grave" site.
>
> My grandfather conducted a ceremony in memory of the

Brave of the Wind in which he made us dance around with
blankets covering ourselves. I was embarrassed! The event
is still available on old movie film. The "narrows" near the
gravesite provide a great place to run a canoe at riptide. I
could always picture Indians enjoying the ride through the
narrows.

My grandfather Nitzsche loved to write articles of historical significance. He had a gift for writing, and he tended
to enhance events with a fine imagination. The legend probably was such an exercise. He took the information related
by Belcher Howard, a good storyteller in his own right, and
enhanced it. I always wanted to dig up the grave and look for
bones. I realized, however, the exercise would be futile.

The "narrows" referred to by James is Bray's Narrows, a key
waterway on Deer Isle's Indian canoe route. As for the name Wauch-
ow-sen, Molly Spotted Elk, a Penobscot who had a deep interest
in her people's traditions, has the following in her dictionary of
Penobscot and Passamaquoddy words: "Wochowsen: celui aui fait
souffles les ventes [*sic*] (one who makes the wind)" i.e. the Wind
Bird of Penobscot and Passamaquoddy mythology.

Hard Times for Indians

Moving from fiction to reality, by the 19th century, Indians
in Maine were under considerable stress. For one thing, there
remained a certain residual animosity toward them, left over from
the earlier Indian wars. This in spite of the Penobscots siding
with the colonists in the Revolution. For another, the extensive
clearing of land for farms and for logging destroyed critical habitat
necessary for traditional hunting and gathering. It also, along
with dam building, adversely affected fishing in ponds, rivers and
streams. Moreover, the new settlers directly competed with Indians
for fish and game, further depleting supplies. George Hosmer, in
his history of Deer Isle, provides an example. Traditionally, one
technique used by Native people to hunt ducks was to drive them

ashore when they were molting and could not fly. A favorite place to do this was Duck Harbor on Isle Au Haut; in their canoes, they would surround ducks and drive them into the cove and up on the shore, where they were easily killed. As they did with many Indian practices, the new settlers adopted this one, but on a larger scale. Here is Hosmer's account:

> At one time a very large drive was made, and many [ducks], attempting to walk over the land from the head of the harbor to the southern shore of the island, perished in the woods, where their remains were seen for a long time. Such unrestrained slaughter soon had its effect, and they decreased or sought other places in which they could be free from this wholesale destruction. No drive has been made for perhaps eighty years or more. My informant, the late Captain David Thurlow, a man well known here in his day, was present at several of the "drives," and from him I obtained the information given above. He died in 1857, at the age of 82 years, and they were a common practice when he was young.

The Indian response to their problems was to regroup away from the increasingly populated coast, as at Indian Island at Old Town (a process begun earlier), and to find ways of adapting traditional practices to the new reality of living on the margins of Anglo-American society. For many, this involved seasonal movement between coastal localities and interior villages. Still, some Indians maintained a lower profile, staying put in coastal locations year round. In general, we know less about this latter group than the former.

Porpoise Hunting from Crockett's Cove

One traditional activity that became important for Indian survival in the 19th century was porpoise hunting. As it happened, there was a burgeoning demand for porpoise oil, and a single porpoise would yield an average of six to seven gallons (one 17th-century source reports almost a barrel of oil from one animal). As fuel for many newly built or soon-to-be-built lighthouses, porpoise oil

SHOOTING A PORPOISE.

SPEARING A PORPOISE.

Figures 13. THESE PICTURES, ABOVE AND OPPOSITE, FROM THE NATIONAL ARCHIVES, SHOW PASSAMAQUODDY PORPOISE HUNTERS, ABOUT 1880. TO SHOOT AND THEN SPEAR THE ANIMAL, THE BOWMAN HAD TO STAND IN THE CANOE. THIS REQUIRED GREAT SKILL, ESPECIALLY IF ANY SORT OF SEA WAS RUNNING. Source: Smith 1993:379 and G.B. Goode: *The Fisheries and Fish-*

was unsurpassed: it gave off good light, was unaffected by cold temperatures, and was not smelly or sticky. The oil was also used for greasing both machinery and wool. In addition, a fatty mass at the root of the animal's jaw yielded about a half a pint of high-grade lubricant for watches.

By 1800, one base of Indian porpoise hunting was Crockett's Cove, an inlet on the western side of Deer Isle through which the boundary between the towns of Deer Isle and Stonington runs today. That the cove was a traditional place for Indian activity is indicated by the presence of prehistoric shell middens of considerable depth. In the June 19, 1903, Deer Isle *Messenger*, an item submitted by someone named Barney Berry reported having heard Mrs. Avery Fifield (formerly Sara Lunt) tell of porpoise hunters in the cove. Born in 1786, she would have been 14 years old in 1800. As a little girl, she would watch Indians come into the cove in their canoes loaded with porpoise:

ing Industries of the United States, Section 5: "History and Methods of the Fisheries": Plate 212, Washington: Government Printing Office.

from which they extracted the oil for cooking food and other purposes. It is said the oil is similar to lard when first taken from the porpoise. She watched the red men smoking their long pipes, waiting to eat. The papoose, or baby Indians, were swinging from the limbs of the trees, cozily nestled in their little baskets, while the older children ran races on the shores or indulged in many athletic exercises, for which the red men are so famous.

As practiced in Sara Fifield's time, the Indians went out in 20-foot birchbark canoes, using guns to shoot the porpoises. (Before guns, bows and arrows were probably used for the shooting.) Nicholas Smith, a long-time student of Indian ways, describes what happened next.

> After the porpoise was shot, a canoe was paddled up to it. The bowman killed it with a spear before grabbing it by sticking two fingers of his right hand in the blowhole and holding the pectoral fin with the left hand, hauling it up at least half its length before dragging it aboard, a tricky job when the catch was a large 300 pounder and a good sea was running. Boys were taken out when they were ten or twelve.

Manly Hardy of Brewer, who knew the Penobscots better than most "whites," and who hunted porpoises with them, wrote the following in 1908:

> When the Indians in one canoe killed a porpoise, they "flashed" another canoe. The flashing was done by holding a wet paddle up and letting the sun strike it so as to throw a flash of sunlight that could be seen a mile, the aboriginal heliograph. The canoe flashed immediately gave up hunting and paddled to the canoe which had killed the porpoise, which was thrown into the second canoe to be taken care of.

Although the processing of porpoises was a great deal of work, it was also something of a festive occasion, as suggested by Sara Fifield's recollections. One Penobscot recalled to me his grandmother speaking of children gathering in anticipation of fried porpoise skin, considered a great treat. And beneath the inch of blubber and three inches of fat, below that was good red meat like beefsteak, on which everyone would have feasted. Since a 300- to 500-pound porpoise would provide a lot of meat, the excess would be cut up into strips to dry or smoke, preserving it for later consumption. Bones and other leftovers were returned to the water.

Although many canoes would have come and gone by way of the mouth of Crockett's Cove, not all of those who gathered for the festivities would have come that way. Little known to many is that there was a back way in, from Deer Isle's main north-south canoe route. From Southeast Harbor, Indians probably canoed up Holt Pond to a short carry (at high tide), to the outlet brook from George's Pond (figure 2). Then, as today, a beaver dam would have made this brook canoeable. (Indians often did what they could to promote beaver activity where it made a brook canoeable.) Another short carry over a beaver dam gave access to the pond, from which there was a half-mile carry to the cove. All these carrys may strike us today as inconvenient, but to Indians then, they were standard operating procedure. Even the half-mile carry is no longer than the one routinely used from Walker's Pond to the Punch Bowl. And the route is a good deal more direct than paddling all the way around the south end of the island.

If, as today, George's Pond's brook supported extensive stands of cattail, this would have been an added bonus. This brings us back to those papooses of which Sara Fifield spoke, for the down was used to wrap around infants for warmth. Other parts of the plant were used for other purposes: young shoots were eaten in the spring, dried to be made into flour or eaten in the winter, and boiled to make a syrup. The pollen was used for flour, the small flowers and seeds were eaten, the leaves were used to weave mats, and the stems to make darts and knives. In all, a most useful plant!

Titillating Tidbits

Although our information on local Indians is scant for the next few decades, there are titillating tidbits indicative of a continuing presence. First, we have the previously mentioned 1831 letter to state authorities from Penobscot Lieutenant Governor John Neptune complaining that settlers were obstructing the traditional use by his people of Conary and White islands close by Sunshine. Then, by mid-century, we have this anecdote from Emily (Greene) Gross about her grandmother, Hattie Powers:

> Gram told at another time as a young woman before she was married a young Indian brave used to come to her house to see her and sometimes she would go for a ride in his canoe. He also gave her a pair of earrings. Also at this time Gram's mother always made biscuits and kept them on hand because the Indians would come to the window or door, appearing at any time of day and were satisfied when she gave them a biscuit or two, and would then go on their way.

Hattie Powers was born Hattie Snowman and, for the first eight years of her life (1860–1868), lived in West Brooksville. Her family then moved across the Reach to the north end of Little Deer, near Indian Cove (soon to be renamed Eggemoggin). Hattie lived there with her parents until her marriage to Farrington Powers of North Deer Isle in 1879. It must have been in this interval between 1868 and 1879 that she was visited by her "Indian Brave."

Who were these Indians? Likely candidates are ones known to be active around the Brooksville shores of Smith Cove at the time. Brooksville resident Julie Lubel recalls her father, whose mother was known as a "full blooded Penobscot," speaking of Indians camping at the Mill Pond (figure 3), off Smith Cove. There, they did a lot of clamming and gathered sweetgrass in nearby marshes, carrying their canoes from the Mill Pond to wetlands at the head of Orcutt's Harbor. From this inlet it was but a short paddle across to Indian Cove on Little Deer.

The ancestry of Julie Lubel's Indian grandmother is somewhat enigmatic. There is no reference to her in the records of the Penobscot Nation, but this likely is the result of a fire that destroyed their records. Her maiden name was Ruhamah (sometimes spelled Rohemia) Benson and she lived from 1825 to 1915. Her mother and father appear to have been Margaret Gray and William (sometimes called Witham) Benson, who were married in 1821. As Brooksville historian Walter Snow observes, "data is obscure, and nothing definite has been learned concerning them [William and various other Bensons]. No connection has been established between any of these people in absence of vital records." Two possibilities seem to exist, given Ruhamah's Indian identity: either William Benson was an Indian himself, or Ruhamah was adopted by William and Margaret.

Another glimpse of Indian life is provided by a story about a tan and brown print dress in the collections of the Deer Isle-Stonington Historical Society. Handmade, it was worn by Martha Sylvester (later Holder) when she was about 15 years old. Here is the story:

> In the summer of 1859 the Indians came down the river to gather sweetgrass and frequently came into Sylvester's Cove. One of the Indian women asked Martha, then about 14, if she would make a dress for her and Martha did. In return the Indian woman gave her a sweetgrass basket and a small sum of money. With the money, Martha bought cloth and made this dress for herself.

One other brief mention is this one, from Donald Soctomah's depiction of Passamaquoddy life between 1890 and 1920:

> 1890 Passamaquoddy summer village Deer Island in Penobscot Bay selling crafts to tourists.

I know of no other reference to such a village.

Indians, Baskets, and Rusticators

Mention of crafts, sweetgrass baskets, and sales to tourists brings up another example of the adaptation of old ways to life in a radically changed world. For thousands of years, people on the Maine coast made containers out of bark and other plant materials. These included devices woven from basswood bark, reeds, cattails, sweetgrass, and Indian hemp. By the early 19th century, Indians began to modify this craft to appeal to the desires of non-Indian buyers. The result was production of baskets woven from ash splints. Tough but flexible, these splints were obtained by pounding logs of young brown ash, *Fraxinus nigra*, so as to separate the growth rings. These were then cut to the desired widths. Some baskets were for purely utilitarian purposes; for example, until the advent of mechanical equipment to do the job, the potato harvest in Aroostook county depended on potato baskets made by the Mi'kmaqs. Here on the coast, baskets made by the Passamaquoddies were in wide use in the herring industry, until supplanted by plastic containers.

Fancy baskets, by contrast, although useful in their own ways as sewing baskets, picnic baskets and the like, were made to appeal to the aesthetic tastes of vacationing "rusticators," tourists and other "people from away." Often, vegetable dyes from local plants were used to add color, with aniline dyes coming into use later on. Around 1860, a new weave was introduced, the so-called "porcupine" weave. This was a sharp-pointed weave that was especially popular in the 1870s and 80s. Soon after introduction of this weave, sweetgrass was used along with the ash splints. Finally, "Hong Kong" cord from China was employed as well. By 1900, two-thirds of the residents of Indian Island listed "basket making" as their major occupation, and this had become an important "marker" of ethnic identity.

At first, Indians would sell their baskets door to door, but with the inflow of summer visitors to places like Bar Harbor, they would establish seasonal camps where these outsiders could come to purchase baskets and other craft items. Although Bar Harbor saw the largest encampments, some Indian families went elsewhere, including Deer Isle, Isle Au Haut, and Eagle Island. The great inflow of summer visitors to Mount Desert Island was underway by 1844, but came later to Deer Isle. Steamboat service made the island accessible, however, and by 1880 significant numbers of vacationers were coming to the island. In that year Charles Babson built an inn and cottages on Indian Cove, renamed Eggemoggin, on the north end of Little Deer. A second summer colony was developing about the same time in the Sylvester's Cove-Dunham's Point area (figure 3). In addition, several hotels in Deer Isle and Stonington, not to mention a scattering of families that took in boarders, were available for people looking for relief from the heat of cities and a place to commune with nature. In short, there was a market for Indian basketmakers to tap into.

Unfortunately, Indian activities on Deer Isle proper are not well documented, but they did come. The story of Martha Sylvester's dress is one indication of this, and it is hard to imagine Indians gathering sweetgrass without taking the opportunity to sell at least a few baskets. Even today, there are "old timers" who have recollections of Native people coming down to gather sweetgrass at various places around the island. In a 1995 interview, Carol Billings recalled her grandmother, Wilda Gross, speaking of a group of Indians who came to Sand Beach every year, always on the same day. They would stay for two days, camping on a little bar between the beach and Gundalow Cove. The sweetgrass they would tie into bundles and load into their canoes for transport. Other sources included Burnt Cove, Crockett's Cove and Sylvester's Cove. In the latter spot, Penobscots gathered sweetgrass here in the 20th century, and one family that did so came regularly each summer, setting up shop in Sunset for the season.

Indians and Eagle Island

If Indian activities are poorly documented for Deer Isle, they are better documented for nearby islands, including Eagle, Isle Au Haut, and Saddleback. For Eagle Island, we learn from John Enk's book, *A Family Island in Penobscot Bay* that:

A number of the former residents of Eagle Island tell about visits to the island by small bands of Indians beginning in the 1880s. They either witnessed these visits personally or were told about them by their parents or older friends. Not only the Penobscots from the upper Penobscot River Valley and the Old Town area, but also the Passamaquoddies from Pleasant Point, came down the Penobscot River and Bay and along the coast in their canoes and visited certain islands in the Bay . . . These summer excursions were made for the purpose of gathering shellfish, collecting gull's eggs, and obtaining sweetgrass from which to make baskets.

Harold Ball, son of Capt. John Ball, recalls several of the Indian visits. The Passamaquoddies [actually Penobscots], led by Chief Big Thunder, whom Harold came to know personally, landed in Lighthouse Cove and came to the light to get permission from Capt. Ball to camp on the island. They camped east of the spring which is located near Lighthouse Beach. Although the boundary line between the lighthouse property and the Samuel Quinn farm runs through the middle of the spring and the Indians camped on Quinn land, they always got permission to camp from Capt. Ball. Harold Ball also became a good friend of Joe Dana [a Passamaquoddy], whose family was a well-known tribal group.

The Indian chief took Capt. Ball and his wife out for a ride in a large bark canoe. The Indians seemed to relish seal hunting. They speared them as they basked on the rocky shore or nearby ledges. At times, they also killed porpoises. The visits of these Indians must have occurred during the period 1883-1898, the years during which Capt. John Ball was stationed at the light.

Mrs. Erland Quinn, a daughter of Capt. Howard Ball, says that another group of Indians camped at the same site—Point Field, near Lighthouse Cove—at a later date. This visit must have occurred during the period from 1898 to 1913 while her father was at the light. According to her account her mother, Lucy Ball, "used to bake large pans of biscuits for them and the Indians gave us many sweetgrass baskets to show their appreciation." [Shades of Hattie Snowman Powers' account of giving biscuits to Indians on Little Deer Isle.]

Mrs. Laura (Dodge) Brown recalls having been told that the Indians used to kill porpoises with a bow and arrow. In this way they added to their supply of food. They shot the porpoises from their canoes while paddling along the shore. This certainly was quite a feat, but they were reported as being "very good at it."

Clearly, the initial Indian interest in Eagle Island derived from its strategic location for hunting sea mammals and birds. The Lighthouse Cove is the landing spot closest to Hardhead Island, a short distance east of Eagle, where gulls and other birds nest in abundance. There are as well a number of seal haul-outs not far distant. As for porpoises, they are not uncommon in nearby waters today, and on one occasion I have even seen a Minke whale off Butter Island. Availability of sweetgrass, probably in the marshy

Figure 14. THE QUINN FARMHOUSE, WHERE BEGINNING IN 1900 SUMMER BOARDERS WOULD HAVE PROVIDED A MARKET FOR INDIANS SELLING BASKETS. THOUGH THE PHOTO DATES FROM 2006, NOT MUCH HAS CHANGED SINCE 1900. Photo by author.

area around the ice pond a short distance southwest of Lighthouse Cove, was an added bonus. They probably helped themselves to the many wild berries on the island as well.

The later group of Indians referred to by Erland Quinn's wife may have been drawn by a market for their baskets and other wares, afforded by the opening of a summer resort on neighboring Butter Island, which lasted from 1896 to 1915. By 1900, the Quinns had opened their house to summer boarders—up to 40 of them—as well. Bob Quinn, who lives in the house today, remembers growing up in the 1940s with a toy canoe and bows and arrows, gotten from the Indians.

Chief Big Thunder, mentioned in Enk's account, was a well-known figure, not just among the Penobscots. Born in 1827 to a Penobscot mother and a mixed Portuguese/Wampanoag father, he would have been in his late 50s or 60s when at Eagle Island. He was the youngest of eight children; his mother died when he was eight. To survive, he and his sisters took up basketry, and he traveled widely in the Northeast selling them. In the 1840s he spent eight months or so working for P. T. Barnum, and then the next five decades producing, directing and acting in Indian entertainments— then quite popular—all over New England. Besides his career as a showman, he was also a skilled hunter, trapper, canoeist, orator and storyteller. And like his mother, he was well versed in traditional healing methods.

Chief Big Thunder was his stage persona; his real name was Frank Loring. He was big physically—six foot four and 225 pounds—as well as in personality. He spent much of his time in the summers on Mount Desert Island but, as his sojourns on Eagle Island (and, as we shall see, Isle Au Haut) show, he led the kind of mobile lifestyle favored by his people. At age 72, he is said to have embarked on a journey in a traditional bark canoe, dressed in deerskin clothing and with a birch wigwam, his destination:

Figure 15. "Chief Big Thunder" (Frank Loring, opposite) of the Penobscots periodically camped on Eagle Island in the late 1800s to hunt birds, seals, and perhaps porpoises. Photo by Frank Speck, University of Pennsylvania Museum Image 13024.

Washington, D.C. His purpose was to plead with President McKinley to save his people. On the way, he ate nothing but gull's eggs and fish, making fire the old-fashioned way, without matches. But his strength gave out, and he had to turn back, having gotten nearly halfway down the New England coast. Still, he remained active, and two years after this trip, he was elected Lieutenant Governor of the Penobscots, their second highest office. Earlier, he had served as Wampum Keeper and in other positions. Late in life, he served as one of anthropologist Frank Speck's informants for his classic ethnography, *Penobscot Man.* He was still working a few months before his death, on a new Indian play to be performed in Lewiston.

In his storytelling and entertainment, Frank Loring was not averse to exaggeration, and giving his audience what they expected to hear and see. Consequently, some outsiders were inclined to see him as a fraud. This misses the point, for in fact, he was a cultural survivalist. As anthropologist Harald Prins points out: "He understood the importance of his 'Indian' identity, refused to walk the assimilation path, took a critical stance toward the dominant culture, was not above creatively fooling the affluent white folk visiting his humble abode and milking them for all they were worth." Watching the traditional culture bleed from his community, he became Big Thunder, the trickster, engaged in a "subversive strategy of creative resistance in the form of theatrics."

Indians and Isle Au Haut

Another stop on Frank Loring's travels was Isle Au Haut (which Indians called Solikuk—Sulessik in Passamaquoddy—meaning "Place of the Shells"). According to Gooden Grant of Head Harbor:

> Some Indians used to come to the island from Bangor and Old Town Island. A whole crowd of them used to come down in the summer and kill the gulls for the feathers . . . The government came in and put in a law to stop it. That hurt the Indians. It was a big business for them . . . Those

Old Town fellows were good guys. They used to ship those feathers to New York to trim hats. The feathers were as white as chalk . . . Indians still came down after they couldn't shoot the gulls, they came to get porpoises for the oil. I remember Big Thunder . . . I used to borrow his canoe to go up to the pond [about a half mile away]. Mighty tippy. He never minded. A birch canoe was a good boat if there was an Indian in it. Took their canoes right out to Matinicus. I'd never do that.

Gooden Grant was born in 1876, was fishing by the age of 10, and died at the age of 98. The account (recorded in 1972) implies that Big Thunder and his companions were camped on the seaward end of the island, rather than on the thorofare. The location is a relatively convenient one for getting to Great and Little Spoon islands, where gulls and other birds nested in large numbers. As on Eagle Island, the interest was in hunting and fowling, as opposed to the basket trade.

Another account relates to approximately the same period. As reported in the *Island Ad-Vantages* (February 3, 1955):

Many years ago when Mineola [Rich] was a little girl, the Penobscot Indians had a camp on Robinson's Point near the lighthouse [the opposite end of the island from Head Harbor]. Everyone visited them to see their many works of basket making, beads and other works of handicraft. One Indian asked Mineola's mother what was the name of her little papoose. She was told Mineola. All the Indians began to jabber excitedly. This scared Mineola's mother. But the Indians gave Mineola beads, slippers and were very kind to her. Mineola's mother left the tent as soon as possible and went home with her daughter. Later it was discovered that the word Mineola in Indian means "laughing queen." This relieved everyone as it was thought at the time that the Indians might be planning on kidnapping little Mineola. As we all know today, Mineola is very much unharmed down at Isle Au Haut.

Figure 16. THIS PHOTO FROM THE 1890S SHOWS INDIANS PADDLING SEAGOING CANVAS CANOES IN ISLE AU HAUT THOROFARE. BEHIND IS KIMBALL'S ISLAND. AT THIS TIME, INDIANS CAMPED AT ROBINSON POINT WERE PROBABLY SELLING BASKETS TO RUSTICATORS AT "THE LOOKOUT," AT THE OTHER END OF THE THOROFARE. Photo by John C. Turner, courtesy Deer Isle-Stonington Historical Society.

Mineola Rich was born Mineola Bridges, the first born of four children to Hattie Conary and Samuel Bridges. She is listed in Chatto and Turner's 1910 *Register* as "student," which they define as attending an "advanced institution of learning." This means that the incident recounted above must have taken place in the last decade of the 1800s. At the time, the Point Lookout Club, founded in 1880 by wealthy vacationers, was undergoing rapid growth (by 1910 it had over 50 members). Located at the opposite end of Isle Au Haut Thorofare from the Indian encampment, it would have provided a ready market for Indian baskets and other souvenirs.

Indians and Saddleback Island

Besides baskets, Indians sold a wide range of handcrafted items including tubs, broomsticks, axe handles, toys such as small bark canoes and tipis, tom-toms, and bows and arrows, trinkets such as fancy birchbark picture frames, moccasins, snowshoes, and even canoes. And, as the following item from an unidentified periodical reports, "rustic furniture."

Saddleback Island is at present (1898 or 1899) the home of quite a colony of Indians, all of whom are from that highly civilized and cultivated band known as the Pleasant Point tribe, residing in the vicinity of Eastport. They make daily trips to Stonington and their handiwork is being well exemplified by a number of rustic and ornamental chairs, settees, etc., purchased from them by many of our citizens.

They are devoting their time chiefly to the securing of gulls' breasts and such trophies and specimens as will turn over a dollar or two from some of the summer visitors who will be swarming along our romantic shores very soon.

The camp affords a very pretty scene with its unique combination of canvas and verdant canopy secluded among the rocky promontories of the island. There are four canoes each with a crew of two or three braves made up as follows: 1st canoe, Joseph L. Dana, Gov.-in-chief of the Pleasant

Figure 17. "Tom tom" by summer cottage, Isle Au Haut; typical of items sold to summer people by Indians, it probably was purchased from the Indians camped near the lighthouse. Photo by author.

Point tribe, with his son, Lolar Dana, and a partner, Daniel Socovy; 2nd canoe, Sabbatis and Swissin Lolar, brothers, with William Toma; 3rd canoe, Joe Soccabasin and Frank Francis; 4th canoe, Tom Pollis and Tom Loring. They are all genial and jolly fellows, and most of them speak the English language very fluently.

All but one of these names appear in the 1900 census for Pleasant Point at Perry, then ranging in age from 17 to 47. The one whose name does not appear is William Toma, who was probably a Penobscot. Joseph Dana is the same one mentioned earlier on Eagle Island with Frank Loring. It is not surprising to find Passamaquoddies and Penobscots traveling together, for "tribal" affiliations have never been as hard and fast as Anglo-Americans imagine them to be. Today, there is probably not a Penobscot without Passamaquoddy relatives, and vice versa. Joseph Dana was indeed a chief at the time, having been elected governor at Pleasant Point for a four-year term in 1896. Sabbatis Lolar and Joe Soccabasin were police officers, the others being listed variously in the census as "hunter," "picture frame maker," and "basket maker."

The reference to gull hunting recalls Gooden Grant's mention of the same activity on Isle Au Haut, at roughly the same time. To quote from a book, *Gulls*, by Frank Graham, Jr.:

> In 1899, a New York millinery dealer furnished eastern Maine's Passamaquoddy Indians with guns and ammunition to kill gulls of all kinds. The dealers paid 40 cents each for adults, 20 cents for the brown immature gulls . . . It is estimated that 5,000,000 gulls were killed each year for the millinery trade.

Small wonder that gulls became threatened species!

To many, the idea of Indians slaughtering gulls by the millions will come as a shock, as it conflicts with the popular notion of these people living in harmony with nature. To understand the practice, we must consider it in context.

As earlier noted, land clearing for various purposes reduced the habitat necessary to support the game animals hunted by Indians. At the same time, silting of rivers and lakes from increased erosion, coupled with the ecological damage caused by dam building, log

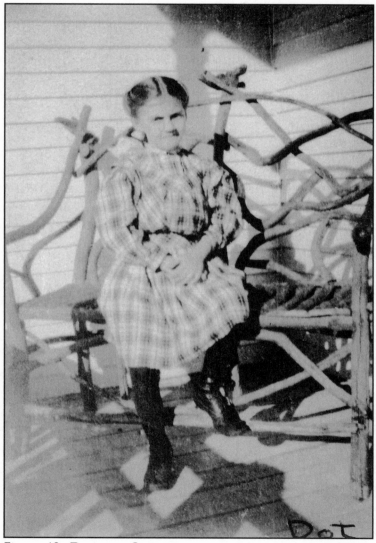

Figure 18. Dorothy Sylvester sits on one of the pieces of rustic furniture purchased from the Indians camped on Saddleback Island. The picture was taken in Stonington, at the end of Rhode Island Avenue. Courtesy of Neva Beck.

drives, and industrial activity, adversely affected fish habitat. Thus, traditional hunting and fishing became increasingly difficult for Maine's Native people. To add to the difficulty, an influx of out-of-state sports hunters and fishers led authorities to realize they could capitalize on the state's natural resources. To do so, they instituted measures designed to protect animals and the remaining wilderness with licensing fees to regulate access and finance the bureaucracy necessary to oversee the operations. In the process, traditional Indian subsistence practices were viewed with disfavor, and eventually criminalized. This despite earlier treaties guaranteeing their hunting and fishing rights.

For people like the Passamaquoddies, things reached a low point in the 1880s when the state of Maine applied its hunting and fishing regulations to them as well as all others in the state. Although this provided jobs for Indians as guides for wealthy sportsmen, it severely curtailed what remained of traditional subsistence practices, making it difficult to get sufficient food for their families. As a consequence, infant mortality skyrocketed on the reservations.

So, the Indians did as any desperate people would do—whatever it took to survive. Given the market for gull feathers to trim the hats of women of fashion in the cities of North America, the mass killing of the birds by Indians should not surprise us; it offered a way to survive in a social world not of their own making.

To sum up the 19th century, "last Indian" stories to the contrary notwithstanding, it is clear that both Penobscots and Passamaquoddies continued to frequent Deer Isle and nearby islands, adapting as best they could to life in what had become, for them, an alien world. In fact, the accounts we have may be the proverbial "tip of the iceberg," as Indians may have been active on many of the islands along the Deer Island Thorofare off Stonington. This is a possibility to which I will return in the discussion of Indians in the 20th century.

IV

The Twentieth Century

Indians and Hog Island

As the last century got underway, Indians kept up their activities on and around Deer Isle. For example, as already noted, they continued to visit Eagle Island perhaps as late as 1913. This may have been the same group that also visited Hog Island, off Cape Rosier. According to the McLanes, "Indians were still coming to the island in the 20th century, searching for sweetgrass for their basketmaking." They may have sold a few baskets as well, as Fred and Amelia Carver who lived on the island began to take in summer boarders—up to twenty—after 1891. To get to Hog, the Indians would have taken a traditional canoe route that crosses Cape Rosier from behind Holbrook Island. Passing through Goose Falls (Edali-Chichiquassik—"where there is a very narrow place") into Goose Pond, it leads to a portage to the head of Weir Cove, and out to a passage between Blake Point and Spectacle Island (see figure 3). Hog lies on a direct line between Weir Cove and Eagle Island, about a third of the way along.

Although use of Hog Island by Anglo-Americans goes back to the 18th century, none lived there until 1860. Native use of the island long precedes that, and there is a story about an incident on the island told to anthropologist Frank Speck by a Penobscot early in the 20th century. Attean Orson, Lieutenant Governor of the Penobscots from 1838 until 1874, and famed as a wrestler among his people, was camped out on Hog by himself. In the night, he dreamed he was attacked by a shaman's animal helper, who wished to do him harm. To defend himself, Orson fought all night for his life with what, in the morning, turned out to be a fallen tree. To many, this may seem a fanciful tale, but in traditional Penobscot belief, as among their Abenaki and Etchemin forebears, dreams were not seen as imaginative products of the unconscious, but rather as alternative realities. They believed that a person's vital spirit could be active while the body slept (or was in a state of trance), and that a shaman had the ability to transfer his spirit into the body of an animal bound to his service in order to accomplish certain goals. Thus, this particular story may well stem from an actual event that took place on the island in the past.

Indians and Other Islands:
Pond, Black (by Swan's), and Isle Au Haut

Between Hog Island and Cape Rosier lies Pond Island, and like Hog, Pond has a sizeable shell midden reflecting a long history of Indian use. This use evidently continued in the 20th century, according to the granddaughter of Hilda and Hobart Blake. The Blakes had a home on the shore halfway between the Head of the Cape and Harborside, and in the 1930s and '40s, Indians came there and wove baskets on their front porch. This weaving was done by women, while their men went off to Pond Island to dig clams.

Another island frequented by Indians in the early 20th century was Black Island, this one located east of Deer Isle between Naskeag and Swan's Island. Speculating on why this island was not settled by Anglo-Americans, the McLanes suggest that the reason

> may have been that it was used by Indians during the summer months and so took on the character of a special preserve for them. I have no certain evidence that Indians came regularly through the 19th century, but there is some presumption of it in the abundant reports of their summer visits early in the 20th century. Carlton Joyce of Swans Island remembers as a boy waiting impatiently for the Indians' arrival on Black Island each spring, for he had a friend (Lola) among them.

Lem Robbins, who spent his youth on [nearby] Pond and Opechee Islands, recalls the regular summer visits of Indian Jo, who camped on the southwest shore of Black Island near a spring. These were Tarratine Indians, I believe, and came from the Penobscot River. They came after ash, sweetgrass for their basket weaving, and also for seal oil and skins.

The McLanes are wrong about the Indians being Tarratines who live in Canada's Maritime Provinces and northern Maine, and are known today as Mi'kmaqs. Having come from the Penobscot River, the Indians on Black Island must have been Penobscots.

Isle Au Haut, too, seems to have been a continuing destination for Indians. Ted Hoskins, for example, recalls them gathering grasses and herbs in the 1940s. Who they were, and where they camped, are unknown to me.

Glimpses of Indians on Deer Isle

Returning to Deer Isle itself, Robert Fifield, who was born in 1923, recalled in a 2005 interview:

I remember every summer, Indians coming here. There were several groups of Indians. I don't remember them living here but they'd come down and set up their tents and they would go fishing off the islands. They'd sell baskets as well. There was only minimal contact between the Indian people and the local families living here.

There were several paths to our area that they would take. Typically, they would come across the Reach and go past the western part of the island and go down to Deer Isle village to the salt water pond [the Mill Pond]. They'd go along the pond for a ways and take canoes across it [the Haulover] to the other side of the road, to the Sunshine area, carrying their canoes over land on the eastern part of that island. They'd canoe down to Isle Au Haut and any of the other islands. Most of the Indian activity, though, was before my time. I do remember that they had a little village in Deer Isle, near Sunset. I can remember the wigwams being out in the field there.

Notable in Fifield's recollection is the fact that the old Indian canoe route was still in use, as it had been by then for at least 2000 years.

Sunset seems to have been a focal point of Indian activity in the early part of the 20th century. For example, there is this intriguing entry in the diary of Cassie M. Stinson for August 17, 1910:

> Miss Katie, little Katherine and the nurse girl goes to the fair this afternoon. Miss Kate bought from an Indian man for mamsie and I, a pretty pin cushion in a sweetgrass basket for mamma and a very pretty little birchbark box embroidered with grass for me.

Figure 19. TWO PIECES OF RUSTIC FURNITURE MADE BY AN INDIAN FOR THE SUMMER COTTAGE OF JAMES CROSWELL. THE LARGER ONE MEASURES 22 BY 22.5 INCHES ON TOP AND STANDS 25.25 INCHES TALL. Photo by author, courtesy of Brenda Gilchrist.

Cassie Stinson's family lived in South Deer Isle, but that summer young Cassie was working at the "Buel Cottage," a summer residence at Dunham's Point. The fair must have been the one put on by the Ladies Circle for the benefit of the Sunset Chapel, which was held on the day of the diary entry. Unfortunately, we do not know the identity of the "Indian man." Could he have come from a "little village near Sunset" still in existence in Fifield's time?

Also at Dunham's Point is the house built in 1902 by James Croswell as a summer cottage. Brenda Gilchrist, who lives there today, recalls that her great uncle acquired a set of "rustic furniture" early in the 20th century from Indians. The account she heard was that Indians "made the rounds" of the cottages around the point, building such furniture to order at the buyer's house. She still has the furniture, which consists of four small "end tables" and a larger one, all with legs of small sections of birch with tops of woven birchbark strips. Most likely, other examples still exist in other summer homes in the neighborhood.

Although we cannot be sure, Brenda Gilchrist's and Cassie Stinson's Indians may have been from the same encampment, located not far from Dunham's Point. Brenda thinks it may have been at Pressey Village, but I have been unable to confirm this. A location near Sunset seems more likely. To speculate further, if this was Fifield's "little village near Sunset," could it have been the one to which Passamaquoddies were coming as early as 1890?

Some of the Indians who came to Sunset may have been the same ones who gathered sweetgrass and probably sold baskets on Eagle Island. This is implied by the following account by anthropologist Frank Speck sometime between 1907 and 1918:

> The magic power of song syllables was thought to have a quieting influence upon the forces causing rough water, and also to strengthen the canoe men. A number of years ago an informant (Charlie Daylight Mitchell) was crossing from Deer Island to Eagle Island in Penobscot Bay during a heavy sea. He was in a small canoe in the company of an old man who chanted the following song all the way across. The singer tempered his voice to follow the pitching of the canoe as

it mounted wave after wave. He said that the boat rode the waves much more easily while the old man was singing.

The meaningless syllables are, repeated over and over again:

kwe ha' yu we, ha' yu we hi'
kwe ho' yu we, ho' yu we.

Figure 20. Musical notation for the Canoe Song, sung by Charlie Daylight Mitchell's elderly companion when traveling from Deer Isle to Eagle Island. From Speck 1997:168.

The closest landfall on Deer Isle from Eagle Island is Dunham's Point, with nearby Sylvester's Cove the most sheltered spot with a good beach for landing canoes. Today, this is the route plied by the Eagle Island mail boat, a three-mile run. Though the evidence is slim, Sylvester's Cove may have been a destination on the proposed Weir Cove-Hog Island-Eagle Island canoe route.

Charles Daylight Mitchell was a descendent of a well-known herbalist known as Lewey Daylight/Jackquatis Mitchell. The nickname Daylight comes from the family's reputation as early risers. Born in 1860, Charlie lived all his life on Indian Island at Old Town. Although his father was Penobscot, his mother was French. His wife, Frances Newell, was one of a number of Penobscot women who spoke Indian, but no English. This was in keeping with the role of women as keepers of Penobscot traditions. Because men commonly had to deal with outsiders, they were able to speak English, but in Charlie's case, his French mother spoke no Penobscot, so neither did he. Yet, in spite of their linguistic differences, Charlie and his wife lived successfully enough to raise a family.

Sunset was not the only site of Indian activity on the island. In the collections of the Deer Isle-Stonington Historical Society is a braided sweetgrass necklace, given to a local girl by her Indian playmates. The girl was Ethel, daughter of George and Myra Brown, who lived on the Reach Road about a half mile from Route 15. In Chatto and Turner's 1910 *Register*, Ethel is listed as attending grammar school. (This would have been the schoolhouse across Route 15 from the intersection of the Reach Road. The building still stands, though converted to a garage.) Thus, the necklace must date to around this time. We know who Ethel was (she married John Farrell, Sr.), but who were her Indian playmates, and where did they live?

Another site of Indian activity was the summer colony that had grown up in the late 1800s around Babson's Inn at the north end of Little Deer Isle. In his recollection of summers at Eggemoggin, as the colony came to be called, George Miller, Jr. mentions Indians stopping by twice a summer in the 1920s to sell baskets and beaded moccasins. He says nothing more about them, but I'd guess the Indians were those (or their descendants) who, in the late 1800s, paddled across from Brooksville to stop off at the Snowmans'.

There are hints, too, that Stonington continued to be visited by Indians. Tilden Sawyer, who liked to collect Indian artifacts in the 20th century, told his daughter Evangeline of a visit one fall to Camp Island, across the Deer Island Thorofare from Stonington. There he noticed three spots where the grass was trampled down in circular patterns, each surrounded by what appeared to be holes for poles. He supposed these to be spots where Indians had put up shelters.

Another anecdote comes from Veronica (McGuire) Mollek, who remembers in her childhood (probably ca. 1920) a man she thought was an Indian, named Adam McGaddis. She can still picture him walking the shore at "Clam City" (now Indian

Point Road) wearing a leather hat with a wide brim and ear ornaments that were discs, perhaps of copper. He was said to live beneath a fish market where the present Maritime Café is located. Unfortunately, I have been unable to confirm his Indian identity. McGaddis is not an Indian name, nor does he appear in the records of the Penobscots or Passamaquoddies. It could be that his mother, whose name I do not know, was an Indian. If her husband was a non-Indian, this violated state law, and they had to be careful to avoid arrest. Commonly, such marriages resulted in loss of Native status.

The Lawrence Mitchell Family

Returning to Sunset, there is this item from the Deer Isle *Messenger* of August 30, 1930:

> Chief L. J. Mitchell and family of Oldtown have established their wigwam at Sunset for August as usual and extend an invitation to friends to call and look over their line of Indian goods.

Figure 21. VIVIAN LUFKIN'S HOUSE, AS IT APPEARED IN 2004. THE MITCHELL TENT STOOD BY THE TREE IN THE FOREGROUND. Photo by author.

Figure 22. DEER ISLE *MESSEN-GER* AD, AUG. 3 & 24, 1939.

As this report implies, the Mitchells came regularly to Sunset, and just as the arrival of other summer residents was noted in the local paper, so too was theirs. Here are some examples:

Mrs. Laurence [*sic*] Mitchell and two daughters, Hazel and Gloria, of Indian Island, Old Town, have set up for business on the grounds of Mrs. Vivian Lufkin." (*Deer Isle-Stonington Press*, July, 1937)

The Lawrence Mitchells and Gloria arrived from Indian Island, Saturday, and are occupying a part of Vivian Lufkin's house." (*Messenger*, July 2, 1939)

The Lawrence Mitchells and Gloria arrived Monday to spend the summer at the Vivian Lufkin place." (*Messenger*, July 11, 1940)

Mrs. Lawrence Mitchell and grandson, Larry Archenbeau, of Indian Island, are here to sell baskets. They are staying with Vivian Lufkin. Mr. Mitchell spent the weekend here with his family." (*Messenger*, July 17, 1947)

Their departure was reported in the August 21 issue:

Mr. and Mrs. Lawrence Mitchell and grandson, Laurence Archanbo [*sic*] returned to Indian Island Tuesday.

The wigwam referred to in the 1930 notice (above) was actually a large canvas tent that was pitched by the road in Sunset Village. Mrs. Lufkin's house is still there, just across the road from "Sunset House," and this is where I remember their place of business well into the 1940s. I also remember climbing the apple tree by the

Mitchell tent with grandson Larry Archenbeaud (correct spelling). By 1950, the Mitchells no longer put up their tent, but Lawrence Mitchell (the correct spelling of his name) would make periodic day trips to the island, stopping by the houses of regular customers to sell. This continued up until a few years before his death in 1956.

Evidently, the Mitchells and Vivian Lufkin developed a close friendship over the years. Not only did they share her house, but she was a frequent visitor to theirs. For example, the *Messenger* reported on September 23, 1937, that:

> Mrs. Vivian Lufkin is visiting the Mitchells in Old Town.

And again a year later on October 13:

> Mrs. Vivian Lufkin was a recent visitor of the Mitchells on Indian Island. (*Messenger*, October 13, 1938)

Other reports include the following:

> Mrs. Vivian Lufkin returned home Saturday from a trip to Portland and Old Town. In the latter place she visited the Lawrence Mitchells. (*Messenger*, October 3, 1944)
>
> Mrs. Vivian Lufkin spent last week at Indian Island visiting Mr. and Mrs. Lawrence Mitchell. (*Messenger*, June 19, 1947)

Lawrence Joseph Mitchell was born on the Penobscot reservation in 1883, one of five sons and two daughters of Sarah Susep and Joseph Mary Mitchell, Jr. of the Daylight Mitchell family. All seven children attended the Carlisle Indian School, but Lawrence and his sister Emily were the only ones who returned to Maine.

The Carlisle Indian School was the first, and one of the most notorious, boarding schools established for the purpose of stamping out Indian culture and identity. Located in southern Pennsylvania, far away from what was still Indian country, it was founded in 1879 by Captain Richard H. Pratt, who had been in charge of Indian prisoners at Fort Marion, Florida. The prevailing attitude at the time was that Indians had to conform to Anglo-American culture or be crushed (today, this would be called ethnocide); Pratt's philosophy was, in his own words, "we must kill the Indian in him and save the man." The facility itself was a converted military post where, for 80 years, cavalry officers had trained to fight Indians.

The children in the school were frequently taken by force from

Figure 23. LAWRENCE MITCHELL (1883–1956). Courtesy *Bangor Daily News*.

their parents. Once there, they were not allowed to return home, and communication with their families was discouraged. Their clothes and other belongings were stripped from them, their hair was cut, and they were dressed in military-style uniforms (boys) or Victorian garb (girls). They were forbidden to speak their own language, whether or not they knew any English. Discipline was harsh: lashing with a leather belt was not uncommon, and a mild punishment for saying something in an Indian language was to have one's mouth washed out with soap. In every way, Indians were depicted as evil, heathenish and savage. Not surprisingly, many students sickened and died, nor were suicides uncommon. A number of those who got through it all found that they had lost so much of their culture that they were no longer accepted in their home community. Often, they couldn't even communicate with their loved ones. But neither did they feel a part of Anglo-American society.

That Mitchell survived the horrors of Carlisle is a tribute to his strength of character and strong sense of Penobscot identity. But at least the school did provide vocational training, in useful skills

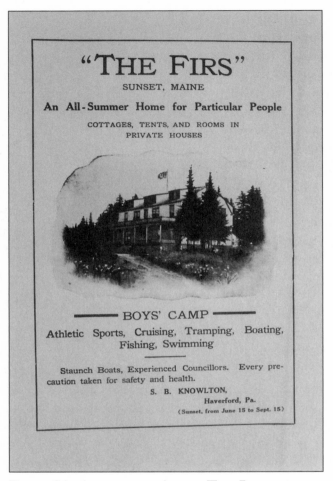

Figure 24. ADVERTISEMENT FOR THE FIRS, A LARGE SUMMER HOTEL IN SUNSET, WHICH PROVIDED A MARKET FOR INDIAN BASKETS AND NOVELTIES. From Chatto and Turner's *Register of the Towns of Sedgwick, Brooklin, Deer Isle, Stonington and Isle Au Haut: 1910.*

such as blacksmithing and carpentry. In Mitchell's case, he learned the art of tailoring as well as printing. After leaving the school, he put in three years in the military, on guard duty as a member of the 7th Cavalry Band in the Philippines. His instrument was the saxophone, which after his return to Maine he played in a band on Indian Island.

After his stint in the Army, he went to Wahpeton, North Dakota, where he operated a tailoring business. Thus, he was part of a Penobscot diaspora, as various members of the nation traveled outside Maine for such purposes as performance in vaudeville and other shows (as in the case of Frank Loring, previously mentioned), to participate in athletics (Louis Sockalexis, for example, who played professional ball for Cleveland), or simply to earn a living, as in Mitchell's case.

While out west, in 1908 Mitchell married Dora LaBelle, a Lakota Sioux. This, too, was not unusual for the time, as Maine had an anti-miscegenation law that did not allow Indians to marry non-Indians. Inherited from Massachusetts, the law has never been repealed, though it is no longer in force. As I heard one Penobscot say, "This made it pretty hard to find a spouse among our own people, as eligible candidates were so few in numbers."

In 1917, the Mitchells returned to Maine with two daughters— Florence (born 1909) and Hazel (born 1915). Finding work as a printer, he later became a compositor at the *Bangor Daily News*, a position he held for 30 years. I do not know when they began their summer sojourns at Sunset, but clearly they were following in the footsteps of others, including the previously mentioned Charles Daylight Mitchell, who was first cousin of Lawrence's grandfather. I do know that Lawrence and his family were coming here by 1926. One who remembers them well—especially their daughter Gloria (born 1922), with whom she developed a friendship—is Mayotta Southworth Kendrick. In 1926 she was eight years old, and had 25 cents, with which she bought a basket from the Mitchells. At that time they were camped just north of the Sunset church, across the Dunham's Point road from The Firs, advertised as "an all-summer home for particular people" with a hotel, cottages, tents, and rooms in private houses. Mayotta's family had a summer home down the road just past Sylvester's Cove. Having bought the basket, she later regretted no longer having the money, and asked her parents for more, and was refused, causing a great many tears.

Clearly, the Mitchells were situated in a good place to profit from the summer trade. They were also well located for getting sweetgrass, which they gathered at Sylvester's Cove. Apparently, they had an arrangement with Anna Osterby's family to exchange baskets for the grass.

Another draw to Deer Isle may have been a connection with the area going back hundreds of years. In his research on the Penobscots, Frank Speck found an ancient association between the Mitchell family and this part of the coast. The same was true of the Susep family. Their animal names were, respectively, Lobster and Crab, and they are said to have always lived near the lobsters and crabs.

Their headquarters were at Stockton and near the mouth of the Bagaduce. The Mitchells were one of the last families to subsist predominantly on resources from the sea, and were reputed to be expert seafarers and salt-water canoeists. In short, the Mitchells, and probably Suseps too, are descendants of Etchemin families whose home territory was the region including Deer Isle.

There are others on the island who also remember the Mitchells. Neva Sylvester Beck is one, and she still has a few items purchased from them. She remembers always addressing them as "Mr. and Mrs. Mitchell," rather than by their first names. I recall the same practice, indicative of an attitude of respect. Indeed, the Mitchells were as much a part of the Sunset community as were other summer residents. Accordingly, their socializing was regularly reported in the local paper, as was that of other inhabitants, both year round and seasonal. Here are a few examples:

> Guests of the Mitchells for the weekend were Lawrence Mitchell, Noel Ranco, Joe Boutin and friend, Mr. and Mrs. Shay and two boys. They all enjoyed a fishing trip while here and Hazel Mitchell was high line, getting the most and largest fish. (*Messenger*, September 2, 1937)
>
> The Mitchells entertained guests from Old Town over the weekend. (*Messenger*, September 9, 1937)
>
> Miss Hazel Mitchell of New York is visiting her parents at the Indian camp. (*Messenger*, September 7, 1939)
>
> Miss Hazel Mitchell, Joseph Tucci and Mr. and Mrs. Adam Liss of Mt. Vernon, N.Y., who have been touring Maine,

Figure 25. THIS SPOT AT SYLVESTER'S COVE WAS A SOURCE OF SWEETGRASS USED BY THE MITCHELLS IN THEIR BASKETMAKING. Photo by author, 2006.

were recent guests at the Indian camp. (*Messenger*, August 15, 1940)

As for work, besides minding the store and gathering sweetgrass, Dora Mitchell gave instruction in basket weaving at Les Chalets Français, the French camp for girls at Mountainville. This could not have been before the late '30s, as the camp did not start up until 1937. My own recollection of the Mitchells is of her as a person of serenity, and him as a friendly man who loved to talk and was good at telling a story. And I loved the toy bark canoes, wigwams, and a tom-tom that we purchased at various times. Sadly, these are now gone, but I still have a birchbark wastebasket with a sweetgrass rim, and two ash-and-sweetgrass baskets. And today, whenever I drive through Sunset, my eyes are invariably drawn to their tent site, and I remember them and the intriguing things they had for sale inside.

The 1937 Guests of the Mitchells

In the previously cited news item from the Deer Isle *Messenger*, the Mitchells played host in 1937 to the Shays, Leo and Florence Nicolar Shay and their sons Charles and Lawrence. She was a daughter of Penobscot Joseph Nicolar, author of the classic *Life and Traditions of the Red Man*. An accomplished basketmaker, she and her husband Leo set up a tent each summer at Lincolnville Beach where, like the Mitchells on Deer Isle, they sold baskets. Though reserved by nature, Florence was an indefatigable activist, working for decades to secure better education for Penobscot children, Indian voting rights, and a bridge from Indian Island to the mainland.

Collaborating with Florence in her advocacy was her sister Lucy, whose more extroverted style complemented Florence's reserve. A well-known Indian performer, Lucy's stage name was Princess Watahwasow. She married a Kiowa, Bruce Poolaw, and the two of them moved back to Indian Island. There, they ran an Indian novelties shop out of a wooden tipi, Chief Poolaw's Tepee, where the bridge comes onto the island. Lucy's nephew Charles has refurbished the tipi as well as the Poolaw house, where he now lives. A veteran of World War II and the Normandy landings, Charles lived for many years in Austria with the wife he met there, before returning to Indian Island. Although he does not remember his family's visit to Deer Isle, which must have been brief, he does remember Gloria Mitchell, whose age was close to his own.

Less is known of the 1937 visitors Joe Boutin and Noel Ranco. The former is not in the genealogical records of the Penobscot Nation, but the latter is. His actual name was Newell Ranco, and he lived from 1876 to 1946. A great-grandson of Newell is Darren J. Ranco, PhD, who was on the faculty at Dartmouth College with a joint appointment in Native American and Environmental Studies, until a recent move to the University of Maine.

"Indian Joe" Lauren

Another news item, this from the Deer Isle *Messenger* (June 15, 1939), reports the following:

> Joseph Lauren, one of the Old Town Indians, is spending some time at the home of Joshua Dunbar. Mr. Lauren is an accomplished violinist. Neighbors of Mr. and Mrs. Parker Eaton gathered at the Eaton home [on Oak Point] last Friday evening, and Mr. Lauren entertained them with many of the modern pieces of music. He also played for dances at Stonington, Northwest Harbor, Oceanville and North Deer.

I first heard of Joe Lauren from Garfield Eaton, who mentioned that his grandfather, Garfield Billings, used to speak of an "Injun Joe" who camped at "Joe's Point" between the Haskell District and Blastow's Cove on Little Deer Isle. I did not connect this individual with Joseph Lauren until I asked Richard Weed, who grew up on Little Deer not far from the causeway, if he knew anything about "Injun Joe." His reply: "Oh sure, Joe Lauren. He was living near the shore behind where Harbor Farm store is now. He used to come up to the house and play the fiddle while mother banged out chords on the piano." This would have been not far from the time when he was staying with the Dunbars.

I have run into one other mention of Joe Lauren, in Lloyd Capen's autobiography. Speaking of his aunt Sarah Marshall, who lived on Quaco Road, Lloyd tells us:

> My fondest memory of Aunt Sarah was listening to her talk with her friend Indian Joe about the beauty of the island. He was always attentive to the thoughts she was sharing as he wove beautiful sweetgrass baskets for sale.

Sarah Marshall died in 1937.

So what do we know of Joseph Lauren? His last name is a variant of the French baptismal name Laurent, a well-known one among Abenakis. Anglicized versions are Laron, Loron, Loren, Lolan, Lola and Loring. The original Abenaki name was Sauguaarum or Sagauarrab, meaning "one who speaks with intent to injure." This implies someone with considerable oratorical skill, whose words carried great power. So it is that, in 1725, we find one Loron acting as chief spokesman for the Penobscots at a meeting in Boston, where he played a major role in shaping the treaty that ended Dummer's, or Lovewell's, War (1721-1726). We last hear of this Loron in 1773 when, no longer a chief, he was hunting moose with crews in one or two other canoes. As Nicholas Smith tells the story:

> Loron was in the head canoe chasing a moose across the Penobscot near Castine when a young hunter in a following canoe shot and killed him, mistaking him for the moose. There was no priest for the Penobscot at that time so the Indians cut off one of his hands, salted and smoked it, and carried it to the priest at Odanak [site of the St. Francis mission in Canada] as was their custom. The priest buried the hand. The hand symbolized Loron's body at the funeral Mass. The hand easy to transport and no odor.

A later Joe Loron was one of four Indians who signed the previously noted complaint in 1776 about "Englishmen from Deer Isle" hunting near the Union River. On the document, his name appears as Roran, as whoever transcribed the words of the petitioners did not understand the difficulties Indians had pronouncing Ls and Rs. Either he or another Joseph Loring (a.k.a. Joe Lolan or Lola) was elected lieutenant governor of the Penobscots in 1810 and served for three years.

Another member of this family who shows up near Deer Isle is Frank Loring (a.k.a. Big Thunder), whose periodic visits to Eagle Island and Isle Au Haut we have already discussed. His descendant, Donna Loring, has served with distinction in the late 20th and early 21st century as the Penobscot representative in the Maine State Legislature. Overall, it looks as if a strong tradition of leadership exists in this family.

As for our Joseph Lauren, we know little about him. Although he is said to be "one of the Old Town Indians," there is no record of him in the genealogical database of the Penobscot Nation. Thus, he must have been living somewhere off reservation. One possibility is a Joseph N. Loring listed on the 1930 federal census for Owl's Head. He is identified as a 52-year-old Indian basketmaker, unmarried, renting a place on his own, and able to speak English. With daily steamboat service from Rockland to Stonington until 1942, he could easily have traveled to the island.

Two other possibilities are Joseph Mitchell Lolar or his son, Josepha [*sic*] M., Jr. The senior Lolar appears in the 1880 and 1899 Penobscot Tribal census and the 1900 Penobscot Indian federal census, so he clearly was an "Old Town Indian." He was born in 1871 or '72, so he would have been in his 60s in the 1930s. His son, born in 1899, would have been in his 30s. Joseph senior is listed in the federal census as a day laborer. His wife, Mary Jane, is listed as a basketmaker. The genealogical records of the Penobscot Nation show her to be a descendant of Joseph Orono and Clara Mitchell. And that is the extent of our knowledge of this family, for after the 1900 census, little Joseph(a) and his parents disappear. They are not noted in subsequent census records.

Whoever he was and wherever he was living the rest of the time, Joe Lauren (or Lolar or Loring) obviously made a number of trips to Deer Isle in the 1930s and perhaps early 40s, staying at several different places (at least two on Little Deer and one on Fish Creek—the Dunbar residence). Like many Indians, he was musically inclined. Both Penobscots and Passamaquoddies boasted brass bands, and Lawrence Mitchell, too, was an accomplished musician. Fiddlers generally, whether Indian or not, were much admired. One of Fannie Eckstorm's stories in her book, *The Penobscot Man*, tells of an incident on one of the 19th-century log drives on the West Branch of the Penobscot. Although a potentially serious jam was forming on the river, all activity stopped when one of the river drivers took out his violin to play a few tunes. Only when he was done did the crew tackle the (by then) major logjam.

The one other thing we know about Joe Lauren is that he was also a basketmaker. Where he sold his baskets is an open question.

In any event, Lloyd Capen's account of Joe's discussions with Sarah Marshall imply that he, like her, had a deep appreciation of the island's beauty.

Rose Dunbar and Fish Creek

As we have seen, when Joseph Lauren came to Deer Isle in 1939, he stayed at the home of Joshua Dunbar. This home, one of five to seven small, tarpaper shacks, stood on the north side of Fish Creek Road, about three tenths of a mile east of its intersection with the Greenlaw District Road. The site is marked today by a small clearing surrounded by spruce woods. As a child, I remember whenever we drove past on a nice summer day, an elderly woman would be sitting on a kitchen chair in the doorway, smoking a corncob pipe. There are others with similar memories, Judy Hill, for one. When she first saw Rose, she was in the doorway of her house with her pipe, wearing a man's grey fedora hat and a ground-length skirt. Her appearance was sufficiently notable to prompt me to ask Francis Williams who she was. His reply: "That's Rose Dunbar, she's half Indian." Some fifty or so years later, I asked Edith Marshall about Rose, to which she replied (without prompting), "She was a Penobscot Indian."

Newman Eaton, a grandson of Gilmore Robbins (who in turn was a grandson of Rose) told me he recalled hearing that Gilmore's grandmother was half to three-quarters Indian and smoked a pipe. Thus, the news item about Joseph Lauren staying with the Dunbars confirms a tie between Rose and other Penobscots. Like Joe Lauren, she does not appear in the Penobscot Nation's genealogical records, probably because her marriage was in violation of state anti-miscegenation law, hence her loss of official Penobscot status.

Rose Etta (or Rosetta—a common name among Indians) Holbrook-Robbins-Dunbar was born in 1866 on Devil's Island, just off Clam City in Stonington, the daughter of Abram Holbrook and his second wife, Lucinda Morey. Lucinda (Lucy) was a daughter of Phoebe Morey, one of a number of individuals living something of a nomadic existence in the mid-1800s among the islands along the Deer Island Thorofare. Dr. Noyes of Stonington described them thusly:

> A larger group of nomads sought a lowly form of livelihood on most of these islands . . . They lived promiscuously mixed up with each other's wives and families that to be specifically mentioned would be out of place here. Not half of these cohabitants were married and a few were the limits of squalor. It was not uncommon for one man to take the other man's spouse and appropriate the same to himself.

As for Phoebe Morey herself, she was the twelfth of thirteen children of Elias Morey, described as

> a hapless drunkard . . . who squandered a considerable property inherited from his father Elijah. Elias's daughters Polly and Phoebe were apparently left to their own devices at an early age and contracted multiple alliances among Deer Isle fishermen—Robbinses, Dunhams and Holbrooks, in particular—which have confounded local genealogists ever since. Dr. Noyes describes Polly with some awe—and, for him, even restraint: "Her career was one of widespread, romantic, sensational, notorious and, finally, of pathetic interest—similar to that of her younger sister Phoebe. She was a strong, wiry character and frequented the clam flats and associated with boating during her early days, the same as the men of her time."

From the tone of these comments, it is clear that these island families—Blacks, Dunbars, Harveys, Holbrooks, and Robbinses—were regarded with a certain degree of disapproval by residents of Deer Isle, raising the possibility that they were not well understood. It does appear, though, that they were living an unconventional lifestyle by the standards of the day.

Although her sister Polly never married, Phoebe did so three times. Her first husband was Mark Robbins; the other two followed Lucinda's birth. As for Lucinda, she was conceived in Mark's absence. When he returned, finding his wife pregnant with someone else's child, he took off for points east and disappeared. Sometime after this (by 1850), Phoebe married Elisha Holbrook, described by Dr. Noyes as "a Frenchman from Cape Cod." Phoebe's third husband, Ed Sargent, need not concern us here.

I have found no evidence of Indian ancestry in the genealogies of either Phoebe Morey or Mark Robbins. Thus, I am convinced that Lucinda Morey's father was an Indian, and that it was from him through Lucinda that Rose Etta Holbrook-Robbins came by her Indian identity. That said, her stepfather, Elisha Holbrook, may have been part Indian himself, as the French in North America freely intermarried with Indians.

Of possible relevance here is that Russ's Island was one of those frequently visited by Phoebe Morey and her compatriots. Originally called Indian Island, the name was still being used at least until 1825. We do not know why it was called this, but one possibility is that it derives from the Indian shell middens on the island. Yet, most islands off Stonington have such middens, but are called by other names. More plausible in my view is that Russ's Island, like several others in the bay in the 1800s, was used by Indians from time to time for encampments. Unfortunately, there is no confirmation of this, but it would put Indians in the right place at the right time for one of them to have a liaison with Phoebe Morey.

Lucinda's first husband, Abram Holbrook, was the son of Lucinda's stepfather Elisha by his first wife. In all, Abram fathered seven children, the first four by his first wife. The oldest of the three he fathered with Lucinda was Rose Etta. At the age of 16, Rose married William Robbins of Belfast. Whistling Bill, as he was known, to distinguish him from several other William Robbinses, was the grandson of James Robbins, who left Deer Isle at the age of 25 to live "down east." James had several children, some of whom returned to Deer Isle, and some of whom (including Whistling Bill's father) moved to Belfast. Born in 1857, Whistling Bill married first Susan Dunbar, with whom he had five children

Figure 26. ROSE DUNBAR AND HER SECOND HUSBAND, JOSH DUNBAR. Photo by Arthur B. Price, courtesy Deer Isle-Stonington Historical Society.

(one, William, Jr., became known as Shackle-Eye Bill). William, Sr.'s second marriage was to Annie Brown of Castine, who left him within a few years. In 1880 he relocated to Deer Isle where, three years later, he married his young wife Rose.

Rose and her husband took up residence on Fish Creek, though they were not the first Robbinses to do so. The pioneer here was Amos Robbins, who bought two acres from Tom Lowe, Sr. He and his wife, Hannah Black, raised their last three children here: Joseph, Daniel, and Hezekiah. As for Bill and Rose, they raised five children, all born on Fish Creek: Allen Rogers (b. 1888), Willard Gilmore (b. 1890), Lillian Ann Frances (b. 1893 but died 1903), Newell Thomas (b. 1899), and Lester (b. 1905). Soon after this last birth, Whistling Bill died, leaving Rose a widow with four children.

In 1907 Rose married Joshua Jerry Dunbar, whose year of birth was the same as hers. Divorced from his first wife, he had no children, nor did he have any with Rose. Josh's mother was Lucretia Morey, second wife of Elijah Dunbar and daughter of Polly Morey, the previously mentioned sister of Phoebe, Rose's grandmother. Lucretia had earlier been married to Hezekiah Robbins, son of

Amos who had pioneered the Fish Creek settlement. Elijah Dunbar also had a house on Fish Creek, across the north branch of the creek from where Josh built his house. Traces of a small foundation on the point between the north and south branches mark the spot today (2005).

Of Rose's children, Willard, Newell, and Lester moved away, the first to Portland and the latter two to California. During the depression, Willard and his family fell on hard times, so they returned to Fish Creek. Later on, Lester, too, returned. Another returnee was Edward Robbins, in 1930. He was the son of William "Shackle-Eye Bill" Robbins and Matilda Ann Dunbar. She was Josh Dunbar's sister; he was the son of Whistling Bill and his first wife, Susan Dunbar (in other words, Rose's half brother). Edward had previously gone to New York City, where he worked on a barge.

Rose's oldest son, Allen, married Ethel Eaton (sister of Willard's wife, Exilana) and raised a large family on the creek. At least two sons, Gilmore and Ralph, stayed in the neighborhood. Also in residence on the creek were Rose's and Josh's mothers, Lucinda and Lucretia. And down the road, at Ox Point, lived one of Hezekiah's sons, Joe.

In the 1930s and early '40s, the people on Fish Creek lived in five to seven tarpaper shacks strung out in a line from Josh and Rose Dunbar's on the west to Gilmore Robbins's on the east. His house, located on the bank at an open spot just before the road goes up a rise into the woods, was the most substantial of the lot. All are now gone, although two root cellars and the posts on which Gilmore's house stood can still be seen.

The people living here, all related in one way or another to Rose, were quite poor and lived a subsistence lifestyle. Their mainstays were clamming and fishing. In a sense, they "owned" the extensive clam-flats in the cove, as no one else would dig there without their approval. The situation was not unlike the traditional Indian hunting territories. These were controlled by families that did not own them in any legal sense, but who had to be asked permission by members of other families who wished to make use of their resources, or even just pass over them. To supplement their living, the Fish Creekers took occasional odd jobs and also received welfare. An oral tradition has it that the town built them a house to live in, but not wishing to all live under the same roof, they disassembled it and used the wood to construct their camps.

Overall, the Fish Creekers seemed to be living something resembling a traditional Indian lifestyle, with their subsistence economy and housing that calls to mind traditional wigwams, with tarpaper replacing bark covering, but with square, rather than rounded, corners. Townspeople's descriptions of the families' children as being "all mixed up together" suggest the Native custom of regarding all children as the responsibility of the entire community, rather than the immediate family alone. This was a measure of the importance they attached to children. Indeed, the community strikes one as akin to the old Indian family band. Overall, the community was not unlike those of Abenakis living in Vermont in the same era.

The attitude of outsiders to the "Fish Creekers" was generally, though not universally, one of disapproval. One expression of this came from Lloyd Capen's mother, who "thought of the . . . tribe as loud, reckless, thirsty drinkers and cussing murderers of the King's English." Other things said of them typically mirror what often was said of indigenous minorities not just in the United States, but by English-speaking people in the colonial world in general. However, those who knew the Fish Creekers best painted a far more positive picture. One outsider who knew them well was Lloyd Capen, who has described them to me as generous, hospitable and willing to share what they had.

In his autobiography, Lloyd Capen describes a visit to Fish Creek as follows:

> We ate baked red kidney beans and hot dogs with brown bread, beets, corn bread and fried apples. Willard's wife Lettie [Exilanda] promoted fried apples in molasses and dumplings in the stews she served every other day. We had either fresh or canned fruit with every meal. "That's how I keep my Willard handsome and healthy," she said. "Next time I go to the store I will stop at Dora Damon's to learn how to butt a braided rug. All the women did in Portland was to end them

in rat tails. If we are going to have a good home, one thing I want is good rugs." She was trying to make me at home when Royal suggested that Lettie write a book about ladies getting together to braid rugs and call it *Rat Tails*. "Watch your young tongue or you will become a wise guy like Ickey," she scolded. I could see how hard they worked to build the shacks for five families and create a small neighborhood between tides [clamming], winter wood cutting and summer service jobs for summer residents. Galen said that when they moved here no natives hired them for labor of any kind. "Why do you think that is?" he asked me. "My guess is that the natives are also do-it-yourselfers who can take care of their own needs as they always have," I said, glad to think of an honest and friendly answer. Had I said that the natives did not trust the clan, it would have been my last tide at the Creek.

Royal had a broken set of Popular Mechanics magazines and three Hardy Boys books for his library and very few clothes. "We can wear our work clothes to the district school, and I get along good there because I can read well and do math fast," he let me know. He said that I would be in grammar school where he would also be in a year. We would be schoolmates for a year before I went to high school. His goal was to own a clam factory like Parker [Eaton] at Oak Point and make it grow. He wanted to learn chemistry and find out if better use could be made of clam and scallop shells than dumping them in driveways.

Even Dr. Noyes, who had a rather harsh opinion of Rose and Josh's grandparents and their goings-on in the islands off Stonington, had complimentary things to say about Josh: he "is a good survivor and very fairminded inhabitant."

As noted, the Fish Creek community was much like contemporary Abenaki communities in Vermont. In these Vermont communities, too, people were closely interrelated, lived in poor, rundown shacks, survived by hunting, fishing, day labor, and public welfare, and households intermingled regularly and

Figure 27. THIS CELLAR HOLE, FILLED WITH BRUSH, IS ALL THAT REMAINS OF ONE OF THE ROBBINS' SHACKS ON FISH CREEK. IT MEASURES 15 FEET ACROSS THE FRONT AND 16.5 FEET FRONT TO BACK, WITH AN ENTRY ON THE FRONT 6.5 FEET SQUARE. Photo by author, 2005.

without formality. Socializing often involved a fiddle player and dancing (recall Joe Lauren, the Indian fiddler, staying with Rose and Josh Dunbar). Outsiders held them in low esteem, and people stayed out of Abenaki neighborhoods unless they lived there. The question must, however, be asked: how much of life on Fish Creek represents a survival in new circumstances of traditional ways, as opposed to poor people simply striving to survive? We can't be sure, but the following incident, again related by Lloyd Capen, at least suggests an Indian worldview:

I was thinking about what Willard had said last night when we were all sitting along the shore watching the moon rise over the water. "Don't tell a soul, but tonight I'm a rich man. All you see around me is mine: the water in the creek, the moon and the evening star, the breeze, my family and we are off welfare at last. None of these treasures can be hidden under a mattress. Someday the clams and all of us will be gone, but the rest will stay and make others feel wealthy with blessings." During the tide, Royal had told me his grandpa often stands out in the rain or in a snowstorm to "feel nature firsthand" as he puts it. "One night when I was little, he took me out of my bed, put me on his shoulders and piggybacked me in the summer rain on the Portland promenade telling me over and over to feel the raindrops on my cheeks."

In sum: given Rose's Indian identity, the focal relationship of all the others on the creek to her, and the similarity of life to that in known Abenaki communities in Vermont, I'm inclined to see life on Fish Creek as owing at least something to values and practices out of Rose's Indian past.

With the death of Rose Dunbar in February, 1946, the Fish Creek community began to break up. This continued over several years as older members died off, and younger members moved elsewhere in search of new opportunities. Today, all that remains on the creek are clearings where the houses of Gilmore Robbins and the Dunbars stood, and two root cellars south of Gilmore's. A third cellar is said to have been located where Ted Hutchinson, a newcomer to the creek, now lives

The Last Sixty Years

With the passing of the Mitchell family and the disappearance of the Fish Creek community, Indians did not themselves disappear from the Deer Isle neighborhood. They were, however, less visible, and so we know less of them. We do know that, in 1959, pulpwood was being cut on Eagle Island by Indian workers. Some of them camped out in a small shack on the edge of the ice pond (the shack is still there). And Bob Quinn notes that when his family was in the scaling business, they used baskets made by Passamaquoddies at Pleasant Point as containers (scales removed from herring were used to make fingernail polish). The baskets were large, with round tops and square bottoms.

As early as 1957, Henry Webb of Sargentville began using

Mi'kmaq "stoop labor" to harvest blueberries on the mainland. After his son took over the business, and as local rakers became harder to find on Deer Isle, he began to use them here as well (in the 1970s). They were Mi'kmaqs, members of the Paul family from Nova Scotia. When the head of that family died, he turned to the Lewey family, a well-known Passamaquoddy family from Pleasant Point. Over time, some Penobscots joined the crews as well. This lasted up to the mid-1990s, by which time commercial blueberrying in this area had become uneconomical.

Other Indians continued to visit the region for other purposes, but it was not always easy, for reasons made clear in the following account: In 1953 or '54, Sylvester Neptune told Nicholas Smith about a trip he took down the Penobscot with plans to go to "the Isle of Haut." Stopping to camp along the way,

> he started a fire to boil tea. The owner of the property smelled smoke and followed her nose to his little campfire. "Don't you know you are trespassing? Fires aren't allowed here. You're going to set my woods on fire." She was completely out of it, as far as a way of life where a person was comfortable canoeing around and camping, making a fire to cook over or even warm himself. I feel that the islands were originally part of a person's hunting territory. They offered a family the opportunity to obtain what the ocean produced and the Indian needed.

Still, some Indians have persisted, including one young member of the Mitchell family. This is what he had to say in a 2004 interview:

> I've canoed the Penobscot from Mt. Katahdin to North Haven five years in a row, which is a 200-some-odd-mile paddle . . . As I'm traveling down the Penobscot . . . I often wonder like how many times I come around a corner and see what my great-grandfather or great-great-grandfather or grandfather might even have seen when they were younger. So I went out and camped out and spent a lot of time out on

Hell's Half-acre [off Stonington] and whatnot . . . canoeing off there and diving in with the porpoises. The water is just so clear there in that area, but very cold.

Almost 250 years have passed since Massachusetts Governor Pownall constructed his fort at the mouth of the Penobscot River to block the Indians' access to the coast and make it safe for English settlement. But as we have seen, both Penobscots and Passamaquoddies have persisted in visiting the region. Their reasons for doing so have varied through the years, but their ties to the region have remained. Let us hope that their visits continue far into the future, and do whatever we can to ensure that they do.

A Note on Names

Each Penobscot had four names:

1. That of his or her family, originally an animal with which they had a close association.
2. A French baptismal name, for example, Michele, anglicized to Mitchell, and Joseph, or Susep as pronounced by the Indians. Although it doesn't happen here, often a son took his father's first name as his own last name, with a suffix denoting "junior" or "eldest son of."
3. A nickname, from some personal peculiarity, odd experience, craving, or distinctive expression. The nickname Daylight, as already noted, came from the habit of rising with the sun.
4. Other names acquired in life as one exploit took precedence over another, or as the name of an older family member was inherited upon the latter's death. In the case of Bashabas, when he became Grand Chief of the Mawooshen Confederacy, he added the definite article in front of his name, as was done for anything preeminent, the best, or largest of its kind.

References Consulted

The Seventeenth Century

In many histories of Maine, as Eckstorm (1945:73) pointed out years ago, there is much confusion over the identity of Indian groups in the state. Even so recent a work as Morey's (2005) *Voyage of Archangell* has it wrong. Eckstorm (1945:73–78) is the gold standard against which all others should be measured; since then, Prins and McBride (2007), in their ethnographic survey of Acadia National Park, have expanded our understanding. Theirs is the most thoroughgoing and reliable consideration of this region's Native people in the period of European contact. I have followed their reconstruction of events closely, supplementing it with information from other sources, including Petersen et al (2004:4–7) on Mawooshen, and Morey (2005) on George Waymouth's voyage. Although flawed by a few errors such as misidentification of the Indians as Abenakis, mistranslation of "Mawooshen," failure to understand that Bashabes was a name as well as a title—see Eckstorm 1945:76—and incorrect location of Bashabes' village, I have accepted his argument that Waymouth's explorations took him into West Penobscot Bay and the lower reaches of the river. Nevertheless, there is a discordant note, which Morey does not confront. This is Waymouth's latitude determination, calculated upon his departure for England. Based upon observations of the sun, under ideal conditions, using all his instruments, Waymouth—an experienced navigator—reportedly came up with latitude 43° 20' N (Gilchrist 1990:16–17). As Gilchrist points out, this would place him in the vicinity of Cape Porpoise, far south of Penobscot country, even allowing for possible errors in Waymouth's calculations. Two possible explanations come to mind: 1. The figures were not published until twenty years after Waymouth's voyage (Gilchrist 1990:16), and may have been garbled by then; 2. Waymouth and his chronicler, Rosier, were cagey about the location of their discoveries, to prevent others from acting independently on their knowledge (Morey, 2005:87n. 102).

Other sources are Haviland and Power (1994:chapter 6) on Indian relations with the French and English throughout New England—see this especially for trade as a diplomatic activity and the significance of weapons exchange in northeast Indian culture; Haviland (2005e) on Deer Isle's Indian canoe route—Biard's 1611 meeting on the Bagaduce is from Prins and McBride (2007) and the jetton is discussed in Haviland (2005e:28); Spiess (1982) and correspondence (1899) between Frank Hamilton Cushing of the Smithsonian Institution and Joseph Williamson of the Maine Historical Society (collection 110 box 2C/9) on the Campbell's Island site; Haviland (2007) on the Deer Isle "war casualties"; Faulkner and Faulkner (1987) on Pentagoet; Eckstorm (1941:xi), Bates (1923, reprinted in Brooksville 1935–36:148–149) Chatto and Turner (1972:15, 26), and Haviland (2006) on the Battle of Walker's Pond. See Prins and McBride (2007:144 n 54 and 145) on the location of the Indian fort, which may have been the headquarters of the regional Chief Madockawando. All quotes are from Prins and McBride (2007), except the one about the 1607 colony on the Kennebec, which is from Haviland and Power (1994:220).

The Eighteenth Century

A shortcoming of conventional histories of Maine is that they either ignore, gloss over, or try to put a positive spin on many actions of early English explorers and settlers. Yet, to understand what was going on between Europeans and Indians, a more objective viewpoint is essential. The most honest account I have come across is Colin Woodard's (2004, see his chapters 2, 3, and 4); this despite his all-too-familiar confusion over the identity of Indian groups. Once you read it, you will begin to understand why the Indians so tenaciously resisted invasions of their homeland by the British.

As in the preceding section, I have drawn heavily from Prins and McBride (2007); all quotes are from them unless otherwise noted. The quote from Duncan (1992) is from p. 148; the inventory of archaeological material from "Agemogen" was provided by Stephen Cox (letter of March 2, 2006, and Cox, 2006). The proclamation of 1756 setting bounties for Penobscot scalps is in Speck (1997:xix). On Meribah Wardwell Eaton, see Hosmer (1905:39–40) and Holden (1979). Material on the troubles over Matinicus is drawn from McLane and McLane (1997:9, 22-23) as well as Duncan (1992:133, 134) and Prins and McBride (2007). As a footnote to the abduction of Ebenezer Hall's family, his wife was eventually repatriated, but his children were not. We do not know what became of them, but often young captives found life preferable among Indians than in the colonies, and that is a possibility here.

The Indian petition of 1776 was kindly provided by Nicholas Smith of Brunswick, who has spent a lifetime studying Maine's Indians. Information on William Greenlaw is from Gross (1980) and the quotes from Hosmer (1905) are from pp. 9, 12. The account of William Eaton's bull is in a file in the archives of the Deer Isle-Stonington Historical Society. Vera Billings was a descendant of William Eaton, and she told this story around 1974. On Seth Webb, see Hosmer (1905:118–119; quoted here) and McLane and McLane (1997:361). His cellar hole was shown me in 2005 by Stan Myers, who then owned the property. My sketch of Joseph Orono is drawn from Eckstorm (1945:52–53, 66, 105, 112, 175) and MacDougall (2004:94–95, 103–104, 110, 111). The opinion that he was the son of a daughter of Jean-Vincent d'Abbadie, Baron de Saint-Castin, is that of Harald Prins (personal communication). His activities on White Island and elsewhere off Sunshine are discussed in Prins and McBride (2007:241–245). Material on John Billings is from Chatto and Turner (1972:26) and Snow (1967, vol. I:20 and II:56); the quote about the Indian garden is from p. 8 of Chatto and Turner. The reference to early settlers digging shot from pine trees at the old Indian village site is Eckstorm (1941:xi). The Carney Island story came to me from Eugene Eaton of Little Deer Isle in 2004 and was published in Haviland (2005c). Although the treaty and story of Swunksus are mentioned in McLane and McLane's (1997:331 and 332) account of Conary's Island, this lacks the fullness of Prins and McBride's (2007:264) account. The story of Greg Merchant and the Indian burial I have heard from several people; all are similar to Capen's (2005:175) version, which is the only one I know of in print. On John Neptune and the Neptune family, see Eckstorm's (1945) classic account.

The Nineteenth Century

The material on the Improved Order of Red Men is quoted in Prins and McBride (2007:335–336); the 1928 source is Harrie B. Coe (ed.) *Maine: Resources, Attractions, and its People, A History*. New York: The Lewis Historical Publishing Co. Vol. 2, pp. 771–74.

The "Last Indian" story which follows, I remember hearing as a boy on family visits to the Nitzsches at the French camp. My source here is Gross (1999) and a letter to me from George James in 2004. On the name Wauch-ow-sen, see Spotted Elk (2003:201).

The discussion of Duck Harbor duck drives (and the quote) is based on Hosmer (1905:17–18). Porpoise hunting from Crockett's Cove is an adaptation from an article by Haviland (2005d). Sources are Gross (2003), Hosmer (1905:107–108 and 151–152) on Sarah Lunt; and Nicholas Smith (1993:372) on techniques used to hunt porpoises (this includes the quote from Manly Hardy). For an article by Manly Hardy on hunting porpoises with a Penobscot companion, see Krohn (2005:279–286). Before they had guns, Indians probably hunted porpoises in much the same way that they hunted whales, as described by Rosier (see Morey 2005:92). The existence of the Holt Pond-Georges Pond route to Crockett's Cove is based on my own inspection of the area; comments on the use of cattails are from Haviland and Power (1994:166).

I owe the next item to Tinker Crouch, a descendant of Hattie Snowman Powers. Hattie's recollection is quoted from a family newsletter. The information on the Brooksville Indians comes from interviews with Julie Lubel (October 13 and November 1, 2006), supplemented by information from Brooksville (1935–36:41) and Snow (1967, Vol III:6). On the transfer of the name Eggemoggin from the south end of Little Deer Isle to Indian Cove at the north end, see Haviland (2004). The story of Martha Sylvester (also courtesy of Tinker Crouch) is the caption for an exhibit at the Sellers House museum of the Deer Isle-Stonington Historical Society. The Passamaquoddy village reference is Soctomah (2002:1). Background material on basket making is derived from Eckstorm (2003:19–30), Prins and McBride (1989) and (2007). Carol Billings first told me of sweetgrass gathering at Sand Beach; her 1995 account is in the archives of the Deer Isle-Stonington Historical Society. Alan Gott remembers Indians gathering sweetgrass at Crockett's Cove when he was young (personal communication 2006), and numerous individuals remember this at Sylvester's Cove.

Quoted material on Eagle Island is from Enk (1973:327–328). I have deleted a line that reads: "Possibly, too, the Pentagoets who live in the region from Castine to Naskeag and were also regarded as a 'seagoing group' visited some of the islands during the early years." This implies a third group, equivalent to the Penobscots and Passamaquoddies, but Enk is wrong about this. As we have seen, Pentagoet was an important gathering place for Etchemins, and a number of canoe routes that allowed Indians to bypass the exposed waters off Cape Rosier took off from there. In historic times, Penobscots continued to use these routes. A direct route from the Penobscot River to Eagle Island passed from Castine Harbor via Goose Falls to the head of Goose Pond, with a short carry from there to Weir Cove and on out into the bay. Enk's "Pentagoets" were undoubtedly Penobscots who traversed this route on the way to Eagle.

I have supplemented Enk's material with a telephone interview with Bob Quinn (November 2005) and an interview in August 2006. The startup date for the Quinn boardinghouse is given in Enk (1973:27); for the Butter Island resort, see McLane and McLane (1997:243–251). The sketch of Big Thunder's life is condensed from Prins and McBride (2007:305–311) and Reilly (2006).

Gooden Grant's recollection of Indians on Isle Au Haut is quoted by Bunting (2000:70). Biographical information on Grant is from McLane and McLane (1997:345) and Pratt (1974:110–112). See Pratt (pp. 11–12) also for Great Spoon Island and its birds. The quote about Mineola Rich is from Gross (2005), with biographical data from Chatto and Turner (1972:240 and 85–86). Information on the summer colony is from the same source, p. 78. On the Indian name for Isle Au Haut, see Haviland (2005a). When I wrote this, I did not question Eckstorm's (1941:99–100) assertion that John Smith's "Sorico" was a corruption of Solikuk, but I now think this is one of the few cases where she was wrong. More likely is Harald Prins' interpretation of "Sorico" as a corruption of "Souriquois"—i.e. "Mi'kmaq Island." Still, I see no reason to doubt Solikuk as the original Etchemin name, and Passamaquoddies still call it Sulessik. Inadvertently left out of my 2005 article is the fact that the end of Kimball's Island with the shell heap, from which I think the Indian name derives, was (before the channel was dredged in 1958) effectively part of Isle Au Haut at low tide, when exposed mudflats joined the two islands. The shell heap itself was of such high visibility in the past that Isle Au Haut resident Ted Hoskins, in a phone conversation in February 2006 described it as standing out "like a white flag."

The Saddleback Island account was brought to my attention by Neva Beck, who shared with me a page from her mother's scrapbook, on which appear the two passages quoted here. The first is also summarized by McLane and McLane (1997:304) and both were discussed in an earlier article by me (Haviland 2005b). Further information on the Indians was provided me by Nicholas Smith (correspondence of April 2, 2005), and some comes from Prins and McBride

(2007:289) and Soctomah (2002:63, 175). The impact of Maine's game laws on the Indians I learned from Donald Soctomah of Princeton, Maine, on a visit to Deer Isle in 2005 (see also Soctomah (2002:25–26 and 112–113) and Bunting (2000:52).

The Twentieth Century

For Hog Island, my sources are McLane and McLane (1997:219) and Speck (1920:271). My interview with the Blakes' granddaughter took place at the Deer Isle-Stonington Historical Society early in 2006. McLane and McLane (1997:442) is my source on Black Island. Finally, my previously noted phone interview with Ted Hoskins is the source of my information on Indians on Isle Au Haut in the 1940s.

Robert Fifield's recollections were the subject of an article by Hunter (2005). Cassie Stinson's diary is in the collections of the Deer Isle-Stonington Historical Society and was brought to my attention by Neva Beck. That the Ladies Circle fair was held on the same day is announced in the Deer Isle *Messenger* for August 12, 1910. Ethel Farrell's necklace, too, is in the society collections (see Haviland 2003:photo 30). Miller's reference to Indian visits to Eggemoggin is (undated– 1993?–:3–4). The account of Charlie Daylight Mitchell and the canoe song is from Speck (1997:167–8), and I am grateful to Nicholas Smith for calling it to my attention. Biographical material on Charles Mitchell is from Speck (1997:305) and Carole Binette of the Penobscot Nation (phone interview, June 2006). Tim Kinchla in the fall of 2007 told me his grandfather's account of possible Indians on Camp Island. Tilden Sawyer's collection of "arrowheads" is now in the Deer Isle-Stonington Historical Society.

I am indebted to Brenda Gilchrist for the opportunity to see, photograph and exhibit a piece of the rustic furniture from the Croswell "cottage." All of my information comes from a telephone interview with her in November 2005 and subsequent conversations.

For Lawrence Mitchell and his family, I have relied somewhat on my own memories, and herein lies a story. When I was working on the first edition of the book, *The Original Vermonters*, in the late 1970s, I wished to acknowledge the influence of Lawrence Mitchell on my career choice. I recalled at the time that his name was Lawrence, but thought I'd better make sure. I remembered my family saying once that he was a chief, so I turned to a list of governors of the Penobscot Nation. There I found a Theodore Mitchell, but no Lawrence. Since the dates for Theodore's term in office seemed to fit, I assumed my memory was faulty. So it was that in *The Original Vermonters* Ted Mitchell was the one acknowledged, a mistake repeated in *Deer Isle's Original People*. It was not until I ran across the news item in the 1937 *Deer Isle-Stonington Press* that I quote in the text (Aldrich 1985:101) that I discovered my mistake, and that I should have gone with my original recollection. The 1930 reference in the Deer Isle *Messenger* to "Chief L. J. Mitchell" explains my confusion. As did many Indian entrepreneurs ("Chief Big Thunder," for example), he seems to have adopted the label for promotional purposes. It also was picked up by his co-workers at the *Bangor Daily News* (1956:18) as a nickname. My parents must have mistaken this for a formal title, which they passed on to me. What I learned from all this is that my long-term memory is a lot better than I thought.

Besides my own memories and the two news items noted above, I have benefited from the memories of Neva Beck, Elsa Zelley, and her son George James, and Mayotta Southworth Kendrick for my sketch of the Mitchell family. Carole Binette, genealogist of the Penobscot Nation, provided genealogical information, and James Francis, Penobscot historian, helped fill in some details. On the origin of the Mitchell family and its ancient association with East Penobscot Bay, see Speck (1997:213 and 217). On the Carlisle Indian School, a brief treatment will be found in Josephy (1994:429 and 433–437). Vivid in my memory is a program in the PBS series *The American Experience*, probably from the 1980s, that delved in depth into this era of Indian education. The advertisement for The Firs is from Chatto and Turner (1910:inside front cover).

My sources on the Shay family are a telephone interview with Charles in September 2006, a short biography of Florence (Kennedy 2006) and a biography of her sister Lucy (McBride 2002). As a footnote, I still had (in 2007) a pack basket that I purchased from Florence and Leo Shay in the mid-1950s at their Lincolnville Beach tent. I have since returned it to Charles.

The news item on Joseph Lauren is reprinted in Aldrich (1985:118). My knowledge of him (such as it is) comes from the sources noted in the text; the Capen reference is (2005:159). Nicholas Smith's quote is from a letter to me of October 2005; this also is a source for my information on variants of the name Lauren; another is Carole Binette. Also helpful in this is information from Harald Prins (e-mail of October 9, 2005), and also see Eckstorm (1945:112). Bunny McBride kindly supplied me with the U.S. census data on Joseph Loring of Owl's Head, and Joseph Mitchell Lolar and his son.

On Rose Dunbar and the Fish Creek community, I have spent hours in the archives of the Deer Isle-Stonington Historical Society going through Dr. Noyes' histories of the Black, Dunbar, Holbrook, Morey, and Robbins families, as well as his material on the islands off Stonington. As others have found (McLane and McLane 1997:310), figuring out the relationships between them is a major challenge for genealogists. I've also talked at some length with Chandler Barbour, Neva Beck, Lloyd Capen, Genice Chase, Newman Eaton, Judy Hill, Edith Marshall, John Robbins, and Paul Stubbing, all of whom remember the Fish Creek community. (Three of them are actual descendants.) On the original name of Russ's Island, see McLane and McLane (1997:109). The quotes from Capen are (2005:162, 164 and 165).

The similarities between the Fish Creek community and Abenaki neighborhoods of the same era in Vermont has intrigued me for some time. Like the Fish Creekers, the Abenakis had no official status as Indian communities, even though the identity of their residents was known. The comparisons I make here are from the Abenaki Petition for Federal Recognition (1982, especially pp. 80, 87, 89, 91, 92, 98). As for attitudes toward indigenous communities in the colonial world, consider this example from southern Africa, where Bushmen are described as a "promiscuous assemblage . . . without laws and without discipline, abandoned to the utmost misery and despair; base deserters who have no other resources to procure them a subsistence but plundering and crime" (quoted in Gordon 2002). Rather than reflecting reality, it reflects the prejudice of the observer.

Material on the last sixty years is from Enk (1973:328) on Eagle Island, supplemented in a telephone interview with Robert Quinn (November 2005) and a second interview in person on the island in August 2006. A telephone interview (November 21, 2005) with David Webb of Sedgwick provided the information on blueberry rakers. The Nicholas Smith quote is from Prins and McBride (2007:355), as is the following quote, which elaborates on information that came to me first hand from the same source. With respect to Hell's Half Acre, it is interesting to note its proximity to Devil's Island. The latter, originally called Island I, had its name changed, according to Dr. Noyes quoted in McLane and McLane (1997:307): "Some of the *better classes*, in honor of the belief that a satanic atmosphere pervaded this region, gave to Island I the name of Devil Island" (italics mine).

Such was a common attitude toward the ancestors of Rose and Josh Dunbar!

Bibliography

Abenaki Nation of Vermont. 1982. A petition for federal recognition as an American Indian tribe by the Abenaki Nation of Vermont. Swanton, VT.

Aldrich, James M. 1985. *A century of island newspapers*. Stonington, ME: Penobscot Bay Press.

Bangor Daily News. 1956. L. J. Mitchell, veteran News employee, dies. August 25–26:18.

Bates, S. L. 1923. The battle of Walker's Pond in the town of Brooksville. *Ellsworth American*, Dec. 31; reprinted in Snow (1967).

Brooksville Historical Society. 1935–36. *Traditions and records of Brooksville Maine*. Auburn, ME: Merrill and Webber.

Bunting, W. H. 2000. *A day's work, Part II*. Gardiner, ME: Tilbury House.

Capen, Lloyd. 2005. *The price of clams*. Ellsworth, ME: Dilligaf.

Chatto and Turner. 1972. *Register of the towns of Sedgwick, Brooklin, Deer Isle, Stonington, and Isle Au Haut: 1910*. Brooklin, ME: Friends Memorial Library.

Cox, Stephen L. 2006. *Report on preliminary archaeological testing of the Scott's Midden Site* (42.82). Deer Isle, ME: Report on file at Island Heritage Trust.

Duncan, Roger F. 1992. *Coastal Maine: A maritime history*. Woodstock, VT: Countryman Press.

Eckstorm, Fannie H. 1941. *Indian place names of the Penobscot valley and the Maine coast*. Maine Studies No. 55, University of Maine at Orono.

———. 1945. *Old John Neptune and other Maine Indian shamans*. Portland, ME: Southworth-Anthoensen Press (reprinted 1980 by University of Maine, Orono).

———. 2003. *Handicrafts of the modern Indians of Maine*. Bar Harbor, ME: Abbe Museum.

Enk, John C. 1973. *A family island in Penobscot Bay: The story of Eagle Island*. Rockland, ME: Courier Gazette.

Faulkner, Alaric, and Gretchen Faulkner. 1987. *The French at Pentagoet 1635–1674*. Special Publications of the New Brunswick Museum and Occasional Publications in Maine Archaeology, Maine Historic Preservation Commission.

Gilchrist, John H. 1990. Latitude errors and the New England voyages of Pring and Waymouth. *The American Neptune* L(1):5–17.

Gordon, Robert. 2002. Dirty words: Nomenclature practices and the African human genome project. Paper presented at a workshop of the African Genome Initiative held at Lanzerae, Stellenbosch, September 16–18.

Gross, Clayton H. 1980. Island settled before 1762. *Island Ad-Vantages*, May 29:4.

———. 1999. The legend of Wouch-ow-sen. *Island Ad-Vantages*, August 26:5.

————. 2003. Wigwams and canoes at Crockett's Cove. *Island Ad-Vantages*, June 5:5.

————. 2005 Laughing queen. *Island Ad-Vantages*, February 3:5.

Haviland, William A. 2004. Eggemoggin: The case of the moveable place name. *Island Ad-Vantages*, November 24:4.

————. 2005a. Before Champlain: The original name of Isle Au Haut. *Island Ad-Vantages*, May 26:6.

————. 2005b. Chairs, hats, Indians and Saddleback Island. *Island Ad-Vantages*, March 24:4.

————. 2005c. History of Carney Island explored. *Island Ad-Vantages*, October 27:5.

————. 2005d. Indians, porpoises and Crockett's Cove. *Island Ad-Vantages*, December 22 and 29:5.

————. 2005e. Safe passage to the sea: An ancient canoe route at Deer Isle, Maine. *Maine Archaeological Society Bulletin* 45(1):25–30.

————. 2006. The battle of Walker Pond. *The Weekly Packet*, August 10:23, August 17:23, August 31:22.

————. 2007. The strange case of the Deer Isle giant. *Island Ad-Vantages*, January 25:4.

Haviland, William A., and Marjory W. Power. 1994. *The original Vermonters* (revised and expanded ed.). Hanover, NH: University Press of New England.

Holden, Edward F. 1979. Who was Meribah Wardwell's father? *American Genealogist* 55(2)83–85.

Hosmer, George L. 1905. *An historical sketch of the town of Deer Isle, Maine*. Boston, MA: The Fort Hill Press.

Hunter, Joyce. 2005. Robert Fifield—a man who did more than he thought he could do. *Island Ad-Vantages*, September 1:10.

Josephy, Alvin M., Jr. 1994. *500 Nations*. New York: Knopf.

Kennedy, Kate. 2006. *Florence Nicolar Shay, Penobscot basketmaker and tribal advocate*. Old Town, ME: Charles Norman Shay.

Krohn, William. 2005. *Manly Hardy: The life and writing of a Maine fur-buyer, hunter and naturalist*. Maine Folklife Center.

MacDougall, Paulsen. 2004. *The Penobscot dance of resistance*. Hanover, NH: University Press of New England.

McBride, Bunny. 2002. *Princess Watahwaso: Bright star of the Penobscot*. Old Town, ME: Charles Norman Shay.

McLane, Charles B., and Carol E. McLane. 1997. *Islands of the mid-Maine coast (revised ed.): Penobscot Bay*. Gardiner, ME: Tilbury House.

Miller, George L., Jr. Undated (ca 1993). *Eggemoggin revisited*. Manuscript in the archives of the Deer Isle-Stonington Historical Society.

Morey, David C. 2005. *The voyage of Archangell*. Gardiner, ME: Tilbury House.

Petersen, James B., Malinda Blustain, and James W. Bradley. 2004. "Mawooshen" revisited: Native American contact period sites on the central Maine coast. *Archaeology of Eastern North America*. 32:1–71.

Pratt, Charles. 1974. *Here on the island*. New York: Harper and Row.

Prins, Harald E., and Bunny McBride. 1989. A social history of Maine Indian basketry. In *Maine basketry past to present*. Deer Isle, ME: Maine Crafts Association, pp. 5–14.

———. 2007. *Asticou's island domain: Wabanaki people at Mount Desert Island 1600–2000*. Acadia National Park Ethnographic Overview and Assessment. Boston: National Park Service.

Reilly, Wayne E. 2006. Maine's Chief Big Thunder survived via showbiz. *Bangor Daily News*, April 20, p. C9.

Smith, Nicholas N. 1993. The Wabanaki as mariners. In William Cowen, ed., *Papers of the 24th Algonquian conference*, pp. 364–380, Carleton University, Ottawa.

Snow, Walter A. 1967. *A genealogical history of the pioneers of Brooksville, ME*. Manuscript in the archives of the Deer Isle-Stonington Historical Society.

Soctomah, Donald. 2002. *Passamaquoddy at the turn of the century: 1890–1920*. Indian Township, ME: Passamaquoddy Tribe.

———. 2004. *Landscapes, legends and language of the Passamaquoddy people*. An interactive learning CD. Princeton, ME: Skicin Records.

Speck, Frank G. 1920. Penobscot shamanism. *Memoirs of the American Anthropological Association*, 6:239–288.

———. 1997. *Penobscot man*. Orono, ME: University of Maine Press.

Spiess, Arthur E. 1982. A Skeleton in armor: An unknown chapter in Maine archaeology. *Maine Archaeological Society Bulletin* 23(2):31–34.

Spotted Elk, Molly. 2003. *Katahdin: Wigwam tales of the Abenaki Tribe*. Orono, ME: The Maine Folklife Center.

Woodard, Colin. 2004. *The lobster coast*. New York: Viking.

William A. Haviland studied anthropology at the University of Pennsylvania, where he received his PhD in 1963. He is now professor emeritus at the University of Vermont, where he founded the Department of Anthropology. Previously he taught at Hunter and then Barnard College in New York City. He has  done archaeological work in Belize, Guatemala, South Dakota, and Vermont. He studied the bones of kings and commoners at the ancient Maya city of Tikal and carried out ethnographic and ethnohistorical research in Maine and Vermont. His one hundred or so publications include ten books, among these five textbooks, one on Vermont Indians (co-authored with Marjorie Power) and two monographs on work done at Tikal, Guatemala.

Haviland and his wife, Anita, live on Deer Isle, where he serves on the boards of the Deer Isle-Stonington Historical Society and Island Heritage Trust.